99

CW00495559

THE YOUNG CRICKETER'S COMPANION

Kevin Keys

National Library of New Zealand Cataloguing-in-Publication Data
Keys, Kevin, 1952-
The Young Cricketer's Companion / Kevin Keys
ISBN 978-0-473-19054-5

A Createspace Digital Print Book
Printed in 2013 by "Createspace"

Design and format by Kevin Keys 2011

The sources of all photographs used in this book have been acknowledged in the text.

Picture Acknowledgments

Kevin Bryant: introduction, 5, 13, 15, 18, 19, 21, 22, 23, 26, 44, 45, 61, 69, 72, 77, 78, 79, 86, 87, 95, 96, 97, 122, 123, 128, 129.

Kevin Keys: 3, 14, 27, 73, 94.

Thank you to all the members of the Hutt International Boys' School cricket teams (2005-2011) whose action photographs are printed within.

I would also like to thank Heather O'Brien for once again demonstrating her peerless qualities as a proof-reader and Peter Watt and Mark Borthwick for their suggestions regarding the cricket content in the book.

Contents

Introduction

There have been hundreds of books written on the subject of cricket coaching over the past two centuries. This book does not attempt to add to that list. Instead it attempts to provide young cricketers with non-technical tips and techniques to help them develop into successful young cricketers. It also seeks to provide young cricketers with a basic knowledge of the etiquette of the game of cricket

The author is a New Zealand Cricket qualified coach who has had many years' experience in coaching young cricketers, and in selecting and managing club, school and representative teams.

He now specialises in one-on-one coaching and correcting unsafe bowling actions in young cricketers.

Why play cricket?

Why do you play cricket? Research shows that young people decide to play cricket for a number of reasons, with boys having slightly different motivations from girls.

Boys play cricket:

- to have fun
- to do something they are good at
- to learn new skills
- to be physically fit
- to improve their skills
- to compete
- because of the challenge
- to be in a team
- for the excitement
- for the action

Girls play cricket:

- to have fun
- for the team spirit
- to be in a team
- for the teamwork
- to be physically fit
- to learn new skills
- to improve their skills
- to get exercise
- for the action
- for the excitement

(Caderyn Gaskin, 2000, Occupying the Crease, a report for New Zealand Cricket)

Fitness for cricket

How good is your endurance?

If you are a pace bowler you will need a high level of aerobic and muscular endurance in order to perform to your best. If you are a top-order batter keen to bat for long periods, you too will need to have high levels of endurance.

Are you strong enough?

If you are a pace bowler, do you have the necessary strength in your shoulders and arms to deliver the ball at top speed for four to seven over spells? Do you have the necessary strength in your hands, wrists and arms to swing your bat consistently in the right zones for long periods?

Are you flexible enough?

In cricket, your body will have to move in all directions in all aspects of the game. If your flexibility is poor, you will have difficulty in getting into the correct position to perform the tasks demanded of you. This is especially important if you are the team's wicket-keeper. Lack of flexibility often results in poor performance and inefficient or faulty technique. It will lessen your speed and power and may contribute to injuries as your muscles will have to work harder to overcome resistance. Poor flexibility will make you tire more easily.

Are you fast enough?

In cricket the necessity for speed is most evident in fast bowlers, in batsmen when running between the wickets, and in out-fielders when chasing the ball that is heading towards the boundary.

How to improve your fitness

- Go for a long run of at least 30 minutes once or twice a week.

- Ask your coach to establish a circuit-training routine for you at your school or local gym. A basic circuit will target the development of your arms, shoulders, trunk and legs.
- Have your coach design a weight training routine for you. Try to perform it at least twice a week. Use light weights and high repetitions to lessen the possibility of injury.
- Make flexibility training a regular part of your practice and pre-game routines. An increase in strength will not be of much benefit without an accompanying increase in mobility. Your coach will design a program for all team members to perform before practice and matches begin.
- Practise to improve your reaction times. This can be done solo by bouncing a tennis ball off a wall or with devices such as Crazycatch, in groups with the traditional slip-catching cradle and organised training games that focus on speed of reaction.
- Make sure you are an efficient runner. Cricket is primarily an endurance event interspersed with short bursts of speed. Eliminate sloppy habits from your running style such as head wobble and flapping arms which will reduce your speed and tire you more quickly.
- Batsmen need to concentrate on developing flexibility and strength in the wrists and forearms. A strong neck is needed to support the weight of the batting helmet and powerful leg muscles are required for carrying the pads while running between the wickets.
- Bowlers need good wrist flexibility and control. They need a strong and flexible lower back, groin and hamstrings.
- Fielders need endurance for repeated chases, power for long throws, quick reactions for close catching, and flexibility for the bending and crouching that is required when stopping the ball in the outfield.

- Wicket-keepers need the agility and speed of a trained gymnast. They need strong neck and shoulder muscles, power in their thigh and calf muscles and plenty of courage. They need to be especially careful to avoid muscle shortening due to constant crouching by doing regular stretching exercises during the game.

Are you mentally fit for cricket?

How do you deal with anxiety and lack of confidence? How do you maintain your motivation levels? How do you manage to focus your attention, then learn to relax?

Being mentally fit for cricket is as important as being physically fit. You must be able to deal with nerves, with the tension of the game situation, while being confident in your own capabilities. You must not fear failure. You must be able to concentrate on the task at hand, yet be able to relax when the pressure is less intense.

Mental preparation training can be practised for any cricketing activity. Before you score your first fifty or your first century, you must believe that you have the skills to achieve these. Before facing the opposition's demon fast bowler you must have developed a mental plan to enable you to deal with each of his types of deliveries.

You should develop the habit of regularly rehearsing in your mind the processes involved in being successful at the task at hand. As you rehearse these movements in your mind, imagine how your body will feel when performing these skills.

Confidence

Confidence is a personal thing and varies from individual to individual. Nobody is fully confident all the time and the unknown or negative past experiences can always constitute a potential problem to your confidence. This can lead to fear of failure and a wish to avoid responsibility. For example, if you believe you have a problem playing leg spin and you know that your next opponent has two top-quality leg spinners, what should you do? You could try and avoid the problem by asking to bat in a position in the batting order where you are less likely to have to face these bowlers. Or you could regard this as a challenge to be faced head-on, and rehearse for a successful performance. By succeeding in this personal challenge your self-confidence will continue to grow.

Motivation

Cricket is not an easy game to master. In fact there is truth in the belief that no-one ever totally masters the game. Many enthusiastic young cricketers become overwhelmed by a run of disappointing performances and give up the game to go and pursue something less demanding. I hope that you will not be one of these, and that you will be a young cricketer prepared to pursue a search for excellence over a longer period of time.

Some cricketers are motivated by fear of failure, others by the need to achieve and be the best they can be. To maximise your level of motivation, you must develop a plan about what you want to achieve in the game. You should then set about achieving those planned goals, realising that there will be unexpected set-backs along the way and that you will need to regularly revise your plan in order to overcome them. In this way your motivation levels will continue to grow as you achieve positive rewards in the coming months and years.

Concentration

This is a special mental skill which needs to be developed to a high level if you are to succeed as a young cricketer. If you are facing a demanding fast bowler, you need to be able to focus exclusively on the task at hand and not allow factors outside your control such as comments made by the fielding team or the disagreement you had with your brother at the breakfast table to lessen your concentration on the ball that is about to be bowled.

Concentration is all about having what is called an "uncluttered" mind, where your attention is solely on the brief moment of the task at hand. The mention of the briefness of the task at hand is important as you must learn to "switch off" between deliveries and relax your intense level of concentration until it is next required - when the bowler begins running in for his next delivery. Failing to do so will lead to mental exhaustion and a significant lessening of your ability to focus on the next delivery. This switching off is important for all actively involved in the game, bowlers, fielders and umpires included.

Team Spirit

A good team spirit will undoubtedly aid the potential for strong personal performance. Humour will lessen tension and anxiety, appropriate discipline will help focus practice routines. Team warm-up games and collective stretching routines help develop a collective team purpose and a sense of enjoyment belonging to the team. These will lead to a general feeling of both individual and team optimism, leading to all involved being in the right frame of mind in which to play the game.

Injuries

A cricketer who is improperly conditioned (unfit) to play cricket is more likely to suffer an injury than one who has followed a regular fitness training program. This is because tiredness or lack of coordination leads to faulty movements and loss of concentration.

If you are unlucky enough to suffer an injury, make sure that you are fully recovered before resuming training or playing. If you have suffered a muscle strain injury, you must be able to play without pain when the affected muscle has been tested to full stretch. This enforced period of rest should not, however, be used as an excuse to do nothing. You should use it as an opportunity to get fit to play. For example, if you have suffered a broken finger or an injured ankle, you can still exercise to maintain a good level of fitness.

This is especially important for young pace bowlers who suffer from sore backs or side strains. If you suffer such an injury, it is important that you get a respected bowling coach to check out the safety of your bowling action. Many a promising young pace bowler had his career ruined by continuing to bowl after such an injury with an unsafe bowling action.

Cricket is a game where there is a risk of injury. In tables of injury rates it is close behind the contact sports of rugby, league, football and hockey. Ball impact injuries have lessened in the last ten years with the almost universal use of batting helmets and thigh guards by today's young cricketers. With today's emphasis on health and safety it is important that schools, clubs, players and officials do all that is reasonably possible to lessen the chances of injuries.

Some of these requirements include:
- ensuring a flat outfield.
- ensuring good footing for bowlers in their run-ups and delivery strides.
- ensuring artificial pitches are flush with the surrounding outfield.
- ensuring watering outlets are carefully covered and flush with the outfield.
- ensuring outdoor and indoor nets have no holes and the run-ups and crease areas are flat and not subject to slippage.
- ensuring the playing and practice pitches are flat and clear of debris.
- ensuring that players are wearing suitable socks and footwear with good shock-absorbency.
- ensuring that all batsmen wear good quality, appropriate and suitably sized, protective equipment such as batting helmets, leather batting gloves, thigh pads, groin protector (box), and batting pads.
- ensuring that the team's wicket-keeper is wearing good quality, close-fitting wicket-keeping gloves and a mouth guard. It is encouraging to see many young wicket-keepers wearing protective helmets when standing up to the stumps.
- ensuring pace bowlers wear heavy long-sleeved sweaters after completing a bowling spell in order to keep the back and shoulders warm, especially on a cold day.

In Summary

As a young cricketer you should not be given, or be forced to undertake, too rigorous a training routine while you are undergoing your growth phases. The major emphasis should be on acquiring skills and improving technique. Most of you will have achieved sufficient general fitness from your winter sport program and/or your school physical education program.

If you are a young fast bowler, you must listen to any warning signals your body is giving you and avoid over-bowling. Get the safety of your bowling action checked out three or four times a year as it is easy for unsafe, bad habits to creep in without your noticing them. Avoid trying too hard when training indoors on hard surfaces as many a young bowler has developed stress fractures in his teenage years through this practice.

In the off-season

Winter training

In general, you should work on the technical aspects of your game during the off-season, and the tactical aspects during the season. Technical is working on such things as how to bowl the ball (your action) and how to play various strokes. Tactical is where to bowl the ball and where to hit the ball.

Be careful, if you are a pace bowler, not to try too hard on hard, unforgiving indoor surfaces. Work on refining your action and developing rhythm rather than emphasising pace and bounce.

In the month before the start of the season, weather permitting, you will be able to practise outdoors, where you can finish off the technical improvements gained during the off-season.

Playing Indoor Cricket

By all means play indoor cricket as:

- it is fun.
- it is fast paced, some calling it the indoor version of twenty20 cricket.
- it is beneficial to your cricket fitness, agility and reflexes.
- it helps improve the speed of your decision-making under pressure.
- all levels can play together and teams can be mixed.
- it will help you transition to the summer game, with skills honed in the indoor version.

Read about the game

There are dozens of coaching books on the market and in your local library. Take some time in the off-season to read one or two of these. You will learn a lot of tips and advice to help you become a better cricketer.

View coaching videos

Many excellent cricket skills DVDs are on the market and viewing them is an excellent way to improve your technique as you watch international players demonstrate particular skills.

Get a junior umpire's qualification

As you get to the later teenage years you will need to start umpiring your own games. In many competitions it is a requirement that you have a player umpire qualification. Players as young as 12 years of age can gain these badges through attending a series of lectures and passing a straight-forward written exam. Your coach will advise you when these courses are available.

Apart from being a qualified player umpire, you will learn much about the laws of the game that will help to make you a better performer on the playing field.

Set goals for the coming season

Achievement goals provide motivation and can be long term, such as to win the competition or be selected for a rep team, or short term such as winning the next game. These goals need to be realistic and attainable. If you set them too high and do not achieve them, you may lose motivation. Discuss your goals with your coach.

Performance goals are more under your control. An example of this will be to learn to bowl a leg spinner. A performance goal describes the process or actions that lead to achievement goals. Again, discuss these with your coach.

Your goals:

- should be clear and should be written down.
- should be measurable. For example, bowling no more

than one ball per over down the leg side.
- should be challenging but achievable.
- should be flexible. You may become more skilled at not bowling balls down the leg side and may want to re-set your goal to just one leg side delivery every three overs.

Develop your own personal improvement plan based on areas you believe need attention. Again, seek advice from your coach on what areas of your game should be in your personal plan.

Practice

The Purpose of Practice

You go to practice to learn and improve your skills so they become automatic reflexes (via muscle memory). Muscle memory is the body's ability to repeat an action over and over without conscious thought about the action. If you have developed early muscle memories that are faulty in a cricket skills sense, your coach will need to assist you in replacing the faulty muscle memory with the correct habit.

Your coach will have planned out the session for the overall benefit of all the team members, but will probably not have a specific plan for you in mind. It is your responsibility to make sure that you get the most benefit from each of your practice sessions.

Practice should have the atmosphere of a match. When you bat in the nets, concentrate hard on improving your batting. Don't regard it as simply a chance to practise your slog shots against the hard-working bowlers. Treat every bowler as you would in a match, as an opponent trying to take your wicket.

Pay attention

You must want to hear what your coach has to say to you. You must focus on what is being said and being demonstrated, catching every word. Avoid the wandering mind, ignore what is going on around you. Remember that your coach, assuming he did play the game, will have a great wealth of knowledge to help you improve your game.

Be busy

Ensure that you take the opportunity to take part in a high number of repetitions of whatever specific skill you are practising. This could take the form of a specific fielding technique, a particular batting stroke or a certain bowling variation.

Have a personal practice plan

Have your own plan about what you want to achieve at each session. Ask your coach to monitor the particular aspect of your game you are working on. Your coach will be impressed with your motivation. Too many young cricketers attend cricket practice, particularly net practice, as an excuse for social interaction rather than skill improvement. The idle "chit chat" about what you are planning to do on the weekend can wait until a more suitable occasion. If you need to chat to the others, talk cricket!

Informal Practice

Don't disregard the importance of informal practice. You will only get better by repetition. The more the better. Backyard and schoolyard practice is vital. A concrete wall, a tennis ball and a bat is all you need for an informal solo practice.

Before the Match

Pre-match meals

You should eat at least two hours before the start of play. Make sure the meal consists mainly of carbohydrates, which are digested more easily than proteins. Wholemeal bread, pasta, rice, potatoes and salads are all good pre-match foods to feed your muscles with. Avoid fried foods, sugary cakes and drinks, desserts and biscuits.

Fluid intake

When playing a summer game like cricket it is easy to become dehydrated. Drink plenty of water before play begins and at scheduled drinks breaks or lunch and tea intervals because the loss of body fluids can cause fatigue or muscle cramps and significantly decrease your performance. Do this even if you do not feel thirsty as thirst is a poor indicator of the need for fluid replacement. Water, or electrolyte replacement drinks, are best. Avoid cordials, soft drinks or fruit juice.

Be a willing helper

When you arrive at the ground you will want to catch up with the latest gossip with your mates. This is fine and natural, but a lot of valuable time is wasted with this idle "chit chat". The first thing you should do is to offer to help with any pre-match tasks that need doing. These might include putting out boundary flags, setting up a portable scoreboard, helping to remove covers, helping to put up tents or sun shelters, setting out chairs and scorers' tables, and so forth.

Be a self-starter

The second thing to do is to get your pre-match warm-up routine underway before your coach has to remind you. This can take the common form of playing a form of touch football or some other game involving movement and handling a ball. If you have practice nets nearby then make use of these for throw-downs. Whatever form your warm-up takes, impress your coach and manager with your initiative.

Check Your Gear

Have you got all that you need in your gear bag? Your gear bag should contain most of the following:

- Bat – is it clean, has any damage been fixed, is the grip firmly fixed to the handle?
- Practice ball(s) – for use in throw-downs.
- Pads – clean and with no loose stitching.
- Groin Protector (Box).
- Thigh Pad.
- Batting gloves – dry.
- Arm guard.
- Batting helmet with face guard or grill, snugly fitting, light in weight, with chin straps.
- Cricket shoes – clean with all spikes present and firmly screwed in. If you are to play on an artificial surface you will need a pair of rubber-soled cricket shoes. Batsmen will favour shoes with spikes at the front and rubber-treaded heels. Pace bowlers will need shoes with spikes front and back with extra ankle support.
- Cricket Trousers – clean and pressed.
- Cricket shirt – clean and pressed.
- Socks – white.
- Cap – your team or club cap, not that of your dream sports team. If you have been selected for a representative team and have been awarded a cap for that team, wear it only when you are playing for that team. Do not be tempted to display your ego when playing for your school or club team by wearing your representative cap.
- Cricket sweater.

- Water bottle – your own personal bottle.
- Sunscreen.
- Energy snacks.

Arrive in plenty of time

Your coach will tell you what time to arrive at the ground. Plan to be there fifteen minutes before the specified time. If you are regularly driven to the ground by a caregiver, make sure that they clearly understand what time you are required to be at the ground. It is most frustrating for the team coach and captain if their pre-match plans are upset because team members have not arrived by the specified time.

Welcome the visitors

Have a welcoming word for members of the visiting team and their supporters. Point out where they should store their gear, and where the scoring bench and toilets are located.

Batting

Mastering batting

You will probably agree that batting is the most enjoyable and exciting part of the game, but it is also the most difficult to master - especially as you probably have only one chance in each game. Successful batting involves not only knowing how to correctly play all the shots, but even more important, when to play them. This demands fine judgement of the flight of the ball.

You need to recognize very early the flight and line of the ball, and then where it will pitch and how high it will bounce. Only then can you choose which stroke to play and then go through with the stroke to bring bat and ball together through correct timing. This judgement will only come after years of regular practice.

Below are some general tips about batting:

- Batting is fundamentally about scoring runs. Practise safe scoring shots. Note that there is no such thing as a totally safe scoring shot - it's all about minimising the risks. The safest attacking shot is the straight drive, as it is only an extension of the forward defensive shot.
- Defensive strokes are for keeping out straight deliveries that will hit the stumps. In effect, if the ball is not threatening the stumps, it should be left alone or scored off. Letting the ball go is a very safe shot. Never defend a wide delivery. Young players seem to think that every ball needs to be played at - it doesn't!
- A good balanced stance will not guarantee success but it will help. The weight of the body should rest evenly and lightly on the balls of both feet, so that you can move quickly into line with the ball.
- It is difficult to achieve accurate timing when you have an incorrect grip. Make sure you have your bottom hand just touching your top hand, with both hands towards

the top of the handle. Do not grip the bat too tightly with your bottom hand as you will find it difficult to play straight bat shots. Your top hand grip should be firm with your bottom hand loose when playing straight bat shots. You bottom hand should tighten only when playing cross-batted strokes.

- A faulty grip can often be traced to playing with too large or too heavy a bat.
- Most young cricketers tend to bowl short down the leg side, so learn to play the pull to help you score freely.
- If you want to consistently time the ball, don't try and hit it too hard.
- Thoroughly learn the backward defensive stroke. This is the easiest stroke to master and makes it difficult for bowlers to get you out. If you are in difficulty, use this stroke until you have begun to sight the ball.
- In past years the forward defensive stroke was greatly over-emphasised. Players tended to play forward before correctly sighting the ball, which often got them into difficulties by being on the wrong foot. Don't commit forward too soon! Let the ball hit the bat. Loosen the grip to "kill" the ball.
- If anticipated bounce is low, tend to play forward and play back if bounce is expected to be high.
- Bounce will tend to be higher when the ball is pitched shorter. Therefore look to play back to shorter deliveries and forward to fuller deliveries.
- To be a successful batter your head must be in line with the line of the ball. If your head is in the correct position, your feet will also be in the correct position. However, the reverse is not necessarily true, so move your head before your feet.
- If you are having a bad patch with your batting, go back to basics. Have your coaching mentor check out your grip, stance and back lift.

A batter is always on duty

Most of the pleasure spectators gain from watching cricket is given by the batter, and the big difference between the batter and the rest of the players on the field is that the batter is always on duty. Nothing on the cricket field can give more satisfaction than a perfectly executed cover drive for four with the ball "kissing" the grass on the way to the boundary, or a lofted straight hit for six back over the bowler's head. The batter sets the tone for the pace of the game and the enjoyment factor for spectators by the way they go about their task. Remember that full-tosses, half-volleys and long-hops are bad balls and should be hit to the boundary every time, no matter what the state of the game.

Waiting for your turn

No matter what your number in the batting order, be ready for your turn. Have all your gear at hand, be an active watcher by studying the bowlers, fielders and tactics of the opposition. Be close to the captain or coach, so that last-minute instructions can easily be given. However, don't be too early in getting ready. Two batsmen padded up is enough. If you get nervous, stand up and walk around. Be aware that having some nerves is natural; you need to learn to control them.

Bats

Using the correct size bat is vital to your development as a young cricketer. A common error for young cricketers is to purchase a bat that is too heavy, which leads to technique and stroke play being negatively affected. The bat will be the right weight for you if you can play all the strokes with you in control, not the bat in control of you. You can try this simple test to check whether the bat is not too heavy for you: hold the bat out in front of you, parallel to the ground, by only your top hand. If you can do this for more than

30 seconds, the bat is not too heavy for you. This simple exercise can also be used as a method of strengthening your top-hand grip - a vital component of successful batting.

Carefully check the grain of the bat. Narrow grains are preferable to wide grains. Try and choose a bat with a minimum of twelve grains visible. If you are able, bounce a ball on the face of the bat. If the sound you hear is a hard sound, the bat will need more "knocking in" before it can be used. If the sound is softer, you will be able to use the bat more quickly, but it may be more likely to get small cracks or surface dents.

Pads

It does not matter whether the buckles of your pads are on the outside or inside of your leg, as cricketers are divided on this issue. But make sure they are done up and the tabs are hidden away as much as possible, as it is very annoying to be given out caught behind the wicket after the ball has made contact with one of them. Inexperienced umpires are often influenced into making "out" decisions based on noise, rather than what they have seen.

Your pads should fit in a way that you can run naturally. Wearing a thigh pad is essential if you want to be confident in getting into line with the ball. Taking a nasty, stinging blow to the unprotected thigh can often lead to lack of confidence and backing away to leg against quicker bowlers.

Batting Gloves

Batting gloves should fit snugly, but allow you to open and close your hands in a normal fashion. Look for leather palms and full impact protection. Consider wearing batting inners to help soak up moisture and make sure you dry your gloves after play if they have become damp.

The best batsmen

The highest class of batsmen are often not the flashiest stroke makers, they are the ones who make the least mistakes. In other words, they are the best thinkers about their batting. They are well-organised, planning carefully for each innings. They analyse the strengths and weaknesses of the opposition bowlers and are aware of where each fielder is placed. They play within their own limitations, eliminating high-risk strokes from their game. They have an unruffled temperament, never letting the bowler know that they have got them rattled. They hate getting out.

Acclimatising your eyes

While you are waiting for your turn to bat, make sure you sit in the same light as the players are experiencing on the ground. Do not be tempted to sit in the dark confines of the dressing room as you will struggle to pick up the path and bounce of the ball at the start of your innings.

Pass the outgoing batter

Help to keep the game moving by passing the dismissed or retired batter before he/she has left the ground. The time taken for batters to change places is dead time and should be reduced to a minimum.

Taking guard

When taking guard, say please and thank you to the umpire. You never know...... The guard you take is up to you, but be aware that taking middle does bring your legs into line with the stumps and make you more vulnerable to LBW decisions. Taking guard on middle and leg is a common choice and takes the pads away from the line of the stumps. If you are tall for your age, a leg stump guard may be right for you.

Starting your innings

Unless the game situation demands you attack from the first ball, you will have some time to play yourself in. This involves learning about the pace and bounce of the pitch, getting your feet moving, studying what the bowler is doing, focusing your eyes on the ball and so forth. Learn to leave deliveries that are not threatening your stumps and play in the "V" with a straight bat to cut down the risk factors. If, for the first few overs, you aim to play with a dead straight bat in front of the wicket, you will almost certainly still be batting and starting to find the ball becoming easier to see and judge.

It is important, however, not to allow yourself to get bogged down as this will give the bowler a psychological advantage over you. Start by looking for singles to get your run tally underway. If your batting partner has been at the wicket for some time, play a supporting role, remembering though that a bad ball is a bad ball whenever it is delivered and it should be despatched to the boundary if it can be done so with a straight bat, even if it is the first ball you have faced in your innings.

Memorize the gaps in the field. As you build your innings assess the wicket, the influence of the weather, the standard and types of bowling, and the standard of fielding.

Study the fielders

Even if you have not been on strike for a couple of overs, this need not be a dull time for you. You should be closely studying the fielders, observing who has strong or weak throwing arms, who is left or right-handed, who is particularly agile and who is slow or quick to get to the ball. Many extra runs can be gained by taking advantage of any lack of skill or urgency by a fielder and many a run-out can be avoided when non-striking batsmen are observant of such factors as mentioned above.

The state of the wicket

If the wicket is hard and fast, with little sideways movement, play forward when in doubt as this will limit your errors. In other words, go back to the short ball, forward to the full or short of a length ball. If, however, you are facing a real speedster, you may be forced on to the back foot to most of his deliveries.

If the wicket is slow or wet, with the ball not coming on to the bat, reverse the approach and play back when in doubt. Look to use the pull or cut if the bounce is consistent.

If the wicket is consistently keeping low, you must favour the front foot, to reduce the chances of being bowled or caught LBW by a "shooter". Try to play straight as much as possible.

If the wicket is erratic in pace and bounce, with one ball keeping low and the next rearing alarmingly, all the previous plans are of little use. You will have to trust your instincts. If the bowlers are exploiting the conditions to their advantage, you may be best to take the game to them by hitting over the infield. This may put them off their previous control of line and length and turn things to your advantage.

Study the bowlers

When facing the real speedster or a medium pacer who is swinging the ball a large amount, it is often advantageous to make your first movement back and across towards off stump to give you a bit of extra time to make your decision. If the ball is short, you continue the back foot movement. If it is full of length, you push forward into what is called the "half-cocked" position. This technique gives you surprisingly more time to see the ball. A disadvantage is that it will reduce your front foot driving opportunities, but it will certainly help you settle down at the start of your innings.

Against all other types of bowlers on good wickets, you are safer on the front foot while you are adjusting to the conditions. If you are facing spinners at the start of your innings, resist the temptation to move out of your crease to the ball. Instead, play yourself in by pushing forward from within the crease, ensuring that you keep your back foot grounded well behind the batting crease. Watch out for the delivery that is full of length, which drifts away. It is easy to overbalance and lift your back foot as you try to drive at the ball.

Hopefully you will have developed attacking shots off both the front and back foot. After getting a start, picking up a number of singles and successfully adjusting to the conditions, it will come to the time when you need to look to play more aggressively.

This is where you have to weigh the risks of each shot against the potential rewards. You should know your capabilities well enough to know which shots you have mastered to a level where they are reasonably low risk and which you have not yet mastered and are too high risk to play unless the state of the game demands them. Often the decision comes down to two choices, higher risk cross-bat boundary shots and deliberately hitting in the air. If you are going to play the cross-bat strokes, the pull and the cuts, you must be sure of the pace and bounce of the pitch. Lessen the risks by not hitting the ball in the air and don't try and hit these shots too hard. Instead, use the pace that is already on the ball and help it on its way to the boundary. In other words, deflect the ball towards the boundary with a turn of your wrists rather than trying to "thrash" it.

If, because of the state of the game or the way the field is set, you must take the aerial route, make sure you are aware where the boundary fielders are placed. Don't be "sucked in" to hitting the ball directly to one of these fielders. If all the fielders in front of the wicket are up, the safest aerial shot is the lofted straight drive. Make sure you go completely through with the shot. Hit it hard, not half-heartedly.

Lastly, try and hit in the air down wind rather than in to the wind. Many a batter has tried to take on a strong breeze only to see the ball "hang" in the air as a fielder manoeuvres under it.

Use soft hands when defending

Relax your grip on the bat when playing defensive shots, especially to slow bowling. This allows the hand to absorb energy from the impact of the ball on the bat and will lessen the re-bound distance of the ball off the bat, lowering your chance of being caught by a close-in fielder or the bowler.

Be an intelligent batter

An intelligent batter will take the game to the fielding team by scoring confidently and freely against all but the most demanding deliveries from the bowlers, but will give few chances for them to dismiss him.

For example, one of his favourite shots is the lofted straight drive which he plays successfully for three boundaries. Not surprisingly, the fielding team captain puts a fielder back on the long-on boundary. The intelligent batter takes account of this and changes his strategy and starts safely picking up singles off virtually every ball by clipping the ball along the ground to the long-on fielder. The intelligent batter keeps the scoreboard ticking over, reduces risk to a minimum, frustrates the bowler and fielding captain, and possibly produces a match-winning innings.

Time to play your shots

Sports scientists have determined that it takes 0.2 seconds to sight, predict the flight of the ball, make a decision on what stroke to play and another 0.3 seconds to play the stroke. This means that for every batter it takes at least 0.5 seconds for the decision and response aspect of playing a stroke. What remains of the time taken for the ball to travel from the bowler's hand to the batter is available for the perception of the ball and the predicting of the flight. A ball travelling at 100 km/h (a typical speed for a 12-14 year-old pace bowler) takes about 0.75 seconds to reach the batter. This means that the batter must sight and predict the path of the ball in the first quarter of its flight. At that moment a decision must be taken and the stroke started. An experienced batter can do this, the less experienced cannot. He needs to see the ball for a much longer period of time to make an accurate prediction and decision.

One way you can help yourself become more skilled at this process is to pick your bat up early, thereby cutting down the movement time in playing the stroke. Another is to combine the pick up of the bat with a first foot movement back and across toward off stump. This will give you a few extra milliseconds to sight the ball. You can still play a successful front-foot shot from this position if the delivery demands it.

As an aside, it is interesting to note that a bowler delivering the ball at 130 km/h gives the batter 0.5 seconds before the ball has arrived at him. This gives the batter 0.0 seconds to see and predict the flight of the ball before deciding what shot to play. Makes you wonder how batsmen cope facing 150-160 km/h deliveries?

Timing the ball

The ball will rebound more forcefully off the bat if struck with the heaviest part of the bat, which is found in the lower half of the bat face. Although we call this sweet spot the middle, it is actually lower down the bat face than the geometric middle.

Taking guard in front of the crease

If you are finding it difficult to score off a pace bowler, with the wicket-keeper standing back, don't be afraid to take guard up to a metre in front of the batting crease. This will serve to disrupt the bowler's rhythm and he will need to adjust his length to avoid bowling full-tosses or half volleys. It will also serve to make it harder for an umpire to give you out LBW as the umpire will have more doubt in his mind as to whether the ball will have continued on to hit the stumps.

Know your limits

Learn your limitations and develop your batting approach accordingly. Every young player will have some weak shots and will need to be wary of playing them and may need to eliminate some entirely. However, your ultimate aim will be to improve these weak shots through practice and correction so that you will be confident to use them in the future. You should aim to work on these weak shots indoors in the winter and in the nets during pre-season practice. You then must decide whether you are confident enough to use them in matches. Your aim should always be to score at the fastest possible rate with the least possible risk.

Upping the run rate

There are stages in a game where it may be necessary to "throw caution to the wind" and take more risks than normal. This does not mean that you have to be reckless and throw your wicket away. However you need to score boundaries, so must have a batting plan for this situation:

- Play each delivery on its merits; do not preplan your stroke before the ball has been bowled.
- Remain relaxed, watch the ball right on to your bat.
- Play regular cricket strokes; don't try and invent a stroke that is not in the coaching manuals.
- Keep your balance and play off a firm base.
- Try to turn the deliveries into half volleys through quick and accurate footwork.
- Maximise your chances of success by playing strokes that you know you have mastered.

Volunteer to open the batting

If you want to learn the art of batting, opening is the best position to be in. You have the following advantages when opening the innings:

- You have less pressure on you to score quickly at the start of your innings.
- You have the longest available time to make a big score.
- Runs are often easier to score because of more attacking fields, a harder ball, and faster bowling, which makes it easier to stroke the ball to the boundaries or past the infield.
- You generally get to face the better bowlers, thereby improving your skill levels.

Backing-up

By the time the ball arrives at the facing batter's end you should be 1-2 metres down the pitch, ready to run. The lesson here is that the shorter the distance you have to run, the less chance you have of being run-out. Be wary, of course, of the straight drive which may risk being deflected by the bowler on to the stumps, so be ready to quickly scamper back into the crease.

Calling

Every delivery should be called, even if it goes straight through to the wicket-keeper. The general rule is that any ball hit in front of the wicket should be called by the striking batter, while any ball hit behind the wicket should be called by the non-striker. There is one exception to this general rule, which is where the ball is hit towards a short third man fielder. The striker knows how fast the ball is moving and is in a better position to know whether the non-striker will be able to make a quick run.

If you are planning to make a quick single, be aware that a batter who has played a front foot stroke is in a better position to accelerate forward than a batter who is deep back in his crease after playing a back foot stroke.
The following general rules apply when calling:

- Do not hesitate. If in doubt go back.
- The first call should be one of "yes", "no", or "wait". Subsequent calls could involve "come one", "one", "look for two", "come two", "come three", "one for the throw".
- If you are the non-striker, watch your partner in the first instance rather than the ball and if he calls for a run obey the call unless it is clearly too risky.
- Do not "ball watch" when you are running away from the ball, as this slows your running speed. Rely on

your partner to communicate to you what is happening behind you. Especially useful here is "your end" to alert him of a throw heading towards the end he is running towards. You can also call out advice such as "look for two".

- If you have a batting partner whom you regularly bat with, you may be able to develop non-verbal signals involving eye contact and small head movements. This will be unsettling to the fielding side and will often catch them unawares.
- As you become more experienced you will find that you will start to know how many runs a shot is worth immediately it leaves your bat.

Running between the wickets

This tends to be the worst skill observed in junior cricket and unfortunately amongst the least coached. Up to 30% of all dismissals in junior cricket are through run-outs.

Do not run on the pitch. There are no exceptions to this rule. Damaging the pitch by running on it will only advantage the bowlers. This means running in straight lines on a single side of the pitch.

The following general rules apply:

- Do not run any unnecessary distance past the batting crease. There may have been a fielding error which was invisible to you, but not to your partner who may call you for an extra run. That extra distance you have just unnecessarily run may cause your run-out.
- Run on a catch. Hope that it will be dropped.
- Run on the other side of the pitch from your partner. The general rule is that the striking batter will run on the off side and the non-striker on the leg side. An exception will be if a left arm bowler is bowling over the wicket to

a right hand batter. In this case both batters will run on the off side, but the non-striker will stand and run much further to the off side so that the batsmen can avoid getting in each other's way.

- If you accidentally get in the way of the bowler or a fielder while running between the wickets, apologise – they have right of way.
- Run the first run as fast as possible. Through this simple technique, ones can often be turned into twos and twos into threes. Make sure you ground your bat just past the batting crease and are prepared to turn for the next run a couple of metres before you reach the batting crease.
- Taking every available run will be most unsettling to the fielding side and can quickly make them rattled. Overthrows, misfields and misdirected bowling often occurs when the fielding side becomes anxious to prevent quick runs.
- If in danger of being run-out, start sliding your bat along the ground a couple of metres before the batting crease. This will make it harder for an umpire to be sure of an "out" decision if it is a close thing.
- Another general rule is "one for the throw". If the ball is way out near the boundary then you should be able to take a run while the ball is in the air on the way back to the stumps. You will of course have studied the fielder's throwing arm and will not be taking the extra run if you know he has a "bullet" arm.
- Very often the more softly you hit the ball, the easier it is to take a quick single. Blasting the ball off the middle of the bat straight to cover or mid-wicket often leads to the error of "running with the shot", with an embarrassing run-out resulting.
- If you drop your bat while running, ignore it and keep running. Get it back after you have completed all available runs.

- Remember - a risky run is not worth anyone's wicket.
- Another good saying to remember is "He who hesitates is lost". This means if you decide to take a run, run hard without hesitation. The split second you take making up your mind is often the amount of time the fielding team needs to run you out.

Behind the bowler's arm

As the facing batter, do not allow yourself to be distracted by any object (or person) that is behind, or passing behind, the bowler's arm. You are quite entitled to ask the bowler's end umpire for the offending object to be removed. Examples would include glare reflecting off a car windscreen or a spectator standing directly in your line of sight.

Averages and Aggregates

Never let your wish for a high average or large aggregate get in the way of your team goals. There is nothing to admire in the exploits of a batter who has made a slow 50 at the top of the order in a limited over game when the bulk of the batsmen haven't had a bat.

Getting Out

Eventually you will get out. When it happens, be a "good sport" and take it well. If the umpire's finger is up, there is nothing you can do about it as there is no decision review system in your grades of cricket. Walk briskly off the field without any show of bad temper or dissent towards an umpire's decision. When you return to your team-mates do not sulk, grizzle, or throw your bat or protective gear. After removing your gear and having a drink, return to your team-mates and show your support to those waiting for their turn to bat.

Finally, reflect thoroughly on your innings and your method of dismissal. What did you do well, what was not so good? From every innings you should learn something. From every mistake you make you should learn something. The lessons learned will be stored in your long-term memory bank, ready to be applied in future innings, so that you will hopefully not repeat the same mistakes.

Reacting to a bad umpiring decision

The umpire's decision is final and must not be criticised, either by word or by body language. An angry or surprised look implies a criticism of the umpire, and must never happen. When you return to your team mates, resist the temptation, no matter how hard it may be, to make negative comments on the umpire's decision.

Applause

If you are fortunate to make 50, or even better, 100, make sure you acknowledge the applause by raising your bat towards the spectators and your team-mates. On your return to your team at the end of your innings, again acknowledge the applause, even if disappointed with the manner of your dismissal. A grim facial expression and lack of acknowledgement are ungrateful and bad mannered and may lead to a stern talking-to from your coach. If your parents are present, they are likely to be embarrassed by your poor behaviour.

Bowling

A tough task

Apart from the wicket-keeper, you, the bowler, have the toughest task of any member of the fielding team. The pitch may not suit your style of bowling, your captain may have asked you to bowl up slope into a strong breeze, the two best batsmen in the opposition are at the wicket and in sparkling form, the ball is soft and not swinging, and you have just had a "sitter" of a catch dropped. How do you respond? As the famous saying says -"when the going gets tough, the tough get going"! You display guts and determination, intelligence and hard work, and remember the basic mantra of "line and length". Remember, a change in your fortunes need take only one delivery.

In order to become a top bowler you must grow to love bowling, and lots of it. You must thrive on the responsibility and be keen to take the ball whenever your captain calls you to the bowling crease. You must have a consistent bowling action which you can repeat under all conditions. You must be able to control where the ball goes, which requires that you learn how and when to consistently release the ball.

You will need to think about your bowling. This starts in the nets when too often young bowlers practise their bowling without giving it any thought. Net practice is the time to experiment, to learn new variations, to concentrate on bowling to a plan. Talk to others, read about bowling, watch great bowlers on television, and always continue to learn.

Do you have the right temperament?

If you want to become a successful bowler you need to develop a bowler's temperament. Having a happy-go-lucky, carefree and good-natured outlook does not sit well with becoming a successful attacking bowler. You need an inner fire which will come to the surface when you have a cricket ball in your hand at the top of your bowling mark.

Practising in the nets

You should be aiming to develop certain skills when you bowl in the nets:

- Accuracy: set aside an over here and there where you tell yourself the length and direction you wish for each ball before bowling it. You will find this difficult at first but will be pleased by your rapid improvement.
- Variations: spend some time with a team-mate away from the nets where you can practise a particular variation over a distance of 8-10 metres. Then spend some time during your net session improving your skill level with the variation in question.
- Concentration: set aside six balls here and there where you bowl to a field you have set in your mind, keeping an honest record of your figures for that over. Repeat at intervals throughout the net session.
- Rhythm: you should be able to do this by "feel". If things don't feel right, ask your coach or a team mate to check you out.
- Building stamina: this can only come from long bowling spells in matches and during practice. Be careful, however, if you are a budding young fast bowler, no to over do it as over-use injury may be the result. Young pace bowlers are limited by competition playing conditions in the maximum number of overs they can bowl in a spell and in a day. Do not exceed these in practice and stop immediately and seek advice if you develop any soreness.
- Spotting strengths and weaknesses in the batter: this process should go on all the time when you are watching, playing or practising cricket.
- When bowling at pace, practise imparting some

backspin on the ball by dragging your index and middle fingers down the back seam of the ball. This backspin will help keep the seam of the ball vertical and will aid your attempts to swing and seam the ball.

So you want to be a fast bowler

Nearly every young cricketer dreams at some stage of being a really fast bowler, hurling the ball down at the batter at blistering pace, watching him ducking and diving to avoid his fearsome bouncers, watching the stumps cartwheel out of the ground or the umpire's finger heading skyward after he has trapped the batter in front with a lethal yorker.

Unfortunately, the ability to bowl really fast is available to only a few who are blessed with the necessary physical attributes of suppleness and flexibility, a fast arm action, a strong back and the ability to develop considerable power through the crease. For the majority of young cricketers speed potential is limited and they need to concentrate on the art of swing, cut, seam or spin to make up for a lack of real pace.

So you want to be a wrist-spinner

This is an ambition to be encouraged as quality wrist-spinners are a rare breed today. There will be many occasions when you will face discouragement and frustration and will be tempted to give up your dream and switch to finger-spin or pace bowling. Try to resist this temptation and stick with it. You are attempting to master the most difficult of bowling arts and the future rewards are worth the short term pain.

Your job will be to take wickets, rather than to restrict runs. You must be aggressive in your approach and look to attack the batter. You will need a supportive coach and a captain who has faith in you and is prepared to use you as a wicket-taker at the possible risk of some expensive overs.

Learn how to bowl straight

A good basic action will enable you to bowl straight. With minor variations it applies to all types of bowling - both fast and slow. Ensure that your bowling action is smooth, safe and efficient. The best way for this to be done is to have your bowling action analysed through video. Modern video cameras are a brilliant coaching tool in cricket, especially in the coaching of bowling. Slow motion and frame-by-frame analysis will enable an experienced coach to identify faults or aspects of your bowling action that need attention.

Learn to run up straight, go through the crease straight, and follow through straight. If you consistently do this, and you have an efficient bowling action, the ball is likely to go straight.

Remember, bowling straight means bowling at the stumps. Eight out of every ten deliveries should be directed at those three sticks. If you think about it, two of the common methods of dismissal require that you bowl straight - bowled and LBW. If you are not consistently bowling straight you are significantly reducing your chances of taking wickets.

Learn how to bowl a good length

This is not a skill that a coach can easily teach. A good coach can teach you to bowl straight, but you, the bowler, will learn the correct lengths with practice and experience. Bowling a certain length requires that you learn the correct release point of the ball from your hand. Bowling with the correct release point is a skill in itself and will take many hours of practice. Hang on to the ball too long and you will bowl too short; let it go too early and it will be too full. Through trial and error you will develop a feel for the correct release point for the length you are trying to bowl.

Bowling a good length usually means making the batter uncertain whether to play forward or back. If you are able to swing the ball, try and bowl at a length that will draw the batter forward to maximise your chances of getting the edge.

A good length ball is one which hits the pitch too far up for the batter to step back to comfortably play it as it rises, but too short for him to play it as a full toss or half volley off the front foot. This may vary from ball to ball, depending on the batter's footwork, and from pitch to pitch if one is dry and the other is damp. A good length ball always gives the batter a minimum of time to know what to do, thus forcing him on the defensive or into taking risks if attempting to play attacking strokes.

Good length varies with the pace you bowl at. A good length ball from a slow bowler will be much closer to the batsman than a good length ball from a fast bowler.

Good length also varies with the height and aggressiveness of the batter. A tall batter can reach forward further than a shorter player, so you will need to bowl a shorter "good" length to the taller player,

The state of the wicket also influences what is or isn't a good length. The faster the wicket the shorter the ball can be pitched and still be a good length.

What should be the length of my run-up?

There is no definitive answer to this question. It is very much an individual choice. In general, it should be as many paces as you need to accelerate to the speed at which you feel balanced and ready to bowl. However, it is true to say that most young pace bowlers use too long a run-up, hoping to intimidate the batter with its length. They miss-stride and waste the entire run-up, tiring themselves out in the process. Common faults to look out for in this over-long approach include skipping, hopping, and shortening and lengthening the strides.

What should I look at?

Certainly not the bowling crease or your footmarks. You should start by looking down to make sure you are starting from the correct marked position, then keep your eyes fixed on the target. What should this target be? The top of off-stump is often used. This has two purposes: firstly, it ensures that you are intending to bowl down an appropriate imaginary line; secondly, sports science has shown that we tend to pitch the ball somewhat shorter than what we are looking at.

Which side of the stumps should I bowl from?

Ninety-nine percent of the time, the answer is simple - over the wicket and as close to the stumps as is comfortable. This will enable you to bowl wicket to wicket rather than at an angle. It will also enable you to gain more movement and maximise your chances of gaining LBW decisions.

Line and length together

Bowling a good line means not only bowling at the stumps, but more accurately, bowling at middle and off stumps. Bowling down the leg side is a "big no" as it encourages attacking shots by the batter, eliminates the possibility of bowled and LBW dismissals, and increases the risk of giving away wides and byes.

Bowling a good line can also mean bowling between the lines of off stump and just outside off stump. This is known as the "corridor of uncertainty" where the batter is unsure whether to play at the ball or leave it alone. This should be your primary target as it gives the batter the fewest opportunities for scoring and gives you the best chance of taking wickets.

As a general rule, try and bring the batter on to the front foot by keeping the ball well pitched up. If the batter is able to get on to the back foot and wait for the ball they will usually find it easier to play as they will have extra time to react to any change of direction or uncomfortable bounce.

A consistently testing line and length places great demands on the concentration powers and skill levels of the batter, and makes it more difficult for him to score freely. You will be constantly battling your mind against his mind, your ideas against his ideas, in the hope that you will out-think him and force him into making a mistake which costs him his wicket.

Pace or spin versus accuracy?

A coach does any budding young fast bowler a major disservice by telling him to slow down for more accuracy. Likewise, in telling a young spinner to spin the ball less for more accuracy. Young fast bowlers who want to bowl fast must be encouraged to do so (providing they have a safe action) even at the expense of accuracy. Fast bowlers are a rare breed and must be encouraged to develop as fast bowlers. Accuracy will come later, while their ability to bowl fast will be retained.

Similarly, young spin bowlers should be encouraged to spin the ball first and worry later about accuracy. Spin bowlers tend to take years to develop their craft, but must always be encouraged to spin the ball hard and aggressively.

Think about your bowling:

- Where am I trying to pitch the ball?
- How can I use the wind direction to my advantage?
- Where should I place my field for each batter?
- What is my stock delivery (the one I can bowl most consistently) and how often should I bowl it each over?
- What variations should I use against a particular batter?
- Which end should I bowl at?
- What is the best length to bowl at for this batter?
- What are the strengths and weaknesses of this batter? Should I attack his weaknesses or should I tempt him into playing one of his strong shots, but "out-fox" him with careful field placings?

Variation (a theoretical over):

- Ball one: your natural delivery
- Ball two: the same
- Ball three: vary your position on the crease
- Ball four: your quicker (or slower) ball
- Ball five: your natural delivery
- Ball six: the same

The above is just an example of a varied over. Try not to plan these too far in advance. Take account of the batter who is facing and his strengths and weaknesses. Experiment with the angle of the seam, your wrist position and grip to establish which position provides the most swing with your particular action. A well-disguised variation from your stock delivery provides extra challenges for the batters. It tests how well they have been watching the ball, their technical skill and their levels of concentration.

Outswing and Inswing?

Be careful here. You may be better off perfecting your natural ball, as experimenting with inswingers if you are a natural outswinger may negatively affect your action, leading to you losing the ability to bowl outswing. Using the off-cutter as your main variation is sensible because it uses an action which is much closer to outswing. Leave learning inswing until later years when your action is set and unlikely to be upset through experimentation.

Take risks

As a bowler you should attack the batter by studying his strengths and weaknesses and then entice him into a false stroke. Feed him deliveries that he plays well to make him over-confident or complacent, then bowl him a delivery that appears the same but is in fact slightly different. Perhaps it is slightly slower or quicker, fuller in length or shorter, a bit wider, or given a bit more air. You will often find the batter walking back to the pavilion with a puzzled look on his face. However, you will know the reason for his puzzlement.

Be a hostile bowler

This does not mean that you are constantly trying to hit or hurt the batter. It means that you regard the batter at the other end as your enemy. The warfare between the two of you is psychological. You must believe in gaining ultimate victory over the batter. However, never let your hostility extend off the pitch and don't become a temperamental performer on it. Glaring at the batter, pulling a face, stamping your feet or throwing up your hands at your dreadful fate when the batter has played at and edged the ball through the slips, is childish and will quickly get you and your team disliked.

Be patient

Be aware that even if the batter looks comfortable, he has been forced to solve one problem after another. Every ball you bowl to him is another problem to be solved and, therefore, a potential wicket-taker. You need to persist, confident that in the end it will be the batter who will falter, not you the bowler.

Use a bowling marker

In order to mark the starting point of your run-up, don't do it by scraping a mark with your spikes, use a bowling marker. They can be purchased from your cricket equipment supplier and should be part of your team's kit bag. If your match has official umpires appointed, they will supply the markers.

Look after the ball

You may be given the task of opening the bowling with the new ball. Keep the ball in as new condition for as long as possible. Polish the ball at every opportunity as the shiny new ball swings more than the dull and soft. Remember that every delivery that the batter leaves is a wasted effort. Make the batter play at every ball, so that you maximise the use of the shine on the ball and the hardness of the seam. The hard new ball will naturally bounce more than the softer, older ball and the ability to generate uncomfortable bounce is one of your main weapons as a bowler.

Keep the seam of the ball dry and clean. If the outfield is damp, use a towel to keep water from getting in to the seam so that it does not swell, lose its shape and become like a piece of soap in the hand. Remove any clumps of dirt or grass from the ball, particularly from the seam.

Setting your field

This is one of the hardest skills to learn and will take lots of study and much careful thought. Take every opportunity to study field-settings used by bowlers similar to you in style in first-class or international cricket.

Remember that when the ball leaves the bowler's hand, he is leading eleven players in attacking the batter, not just one.

Jack Massie said it all in 1926:

> *The bowler decides where he wants his field placed and the captain places his fielders in these positions. Each bowler should be taught right from the start to study this matter of placing his own field to the best advantage for his own bowling, and it is a matter which each individual bowler must study very closely.*
>
> *The most important thing to be borne in mind is that fieldsmen must not be wasted by placing them at random in order to stop the result of bad balls, but they must be placed where they will be most useful for good bowling and the bowler must see to it that he cuts the "loose stuff" down to a minimum......*
>
> *It will not pay as a general rule to plug away at a batsman's weakness the whole time as this will have the effect very often of giving him practice in this particular point with anything but the desired result. It may be found far more effective to go through strength to weakness.* R. J. A. Massie, Bowling, p. 13.

Bowl to your field

You and your captain should have agreed on a bowling plan, which it is your job to carry out. Bowl to the field the two of you have agreed upon. If you think the field needs changing, don't do it yourself as it is the ultimate responsibility of the captain. The captain may have spotted a weakness in the batter that you are not aware of, and although the field that has been set may seem strange to you, it is your duty to bowl to this field to the extent of your ability. The captain, in the end, has the ultimate say, but will be mindful of your wishes and will do his best to accommodate them.

If you are on the attack, crowd the new batter or any who show signs of lack of confidence. You must learn to recognise the major wicket-taking fielding positions for your bowling style and be prepared to change the field as conditions change.

If the batter begins to settle in and attack, withdraw the attacking field and fall back to a more defensive plan, designed to slow the batter's scoring rate. If his partner is more defensive or less capable, resume the attack when he is on strike. Don't give in too easily to total defence.

Bowl on one side of the wicket

This really means bowl on or outside off-stump. As most of your matches will be limited-over contests with little or no margin for error on wides outside leg stump, it makes sense not to bowl there. It is amazing how many junior cricket matches are won by the team that bowls the fewest wides.

Maintain pressure from both ends

Bowlers should work in tandem. It is important for bowlers and captains to understand this. A bowler may wearily slide onto a dressing room bench at the end of a day's play without a wicket to his name, but immensely satisfied with his contribution. How is this? It is because of his consistency and tight-fisted bowling which has caused opposition batsmen to get out to the other bowlers through rash strokes or suicidal running between the wickets.

Look after the pitch in your follow-through

If you bowl close to the stumps, make sure you run off to the side of the pitch as soon as possible after you deliver the ball. The Laws of Cricket do not allow you to run straight down the pitch after delivery because of the damage to the batting surface which will occur from your spikes. Ask your coach to check your follow-through at net practice to make sure that you are complying with the relevant law.

The bowler and his captain

Out in the middle is not the time for lengthy discussions about tactics and field placings. These should have taken place before play. In the event of a disagreement on the field, a sensible captain should allow his bowler to have the final say.

The bowler and his wicket-keeper

Make a friend of your wicket-keeper. He is in the best position to advise you on your bowling, what is working well and what is not working so well.

The bowler and the umpire

The bowler will have to accept the umpire's decisions (opinions) far more so than batsmen or fielders. He will have far more opportunities to feel dissatisfied with decisions that don't go his way. Remember that the umpire is the only one who is both stationary and solely concerned with judging the event that has just occurred. He is in the best place to make a correct decision as to whether the ball would have hit the stumps in an LBW appeal or whether it took the edge of the bat. As the bowler, you are moving and are not in a direct line with the stumps, so will see a different picture from that of the umpire. Accept the decision without dissent, or question, and move on.

Senseless appeals

It is not true to say that it doesn't matter how many appeals you make because it is the umpire's job to make a decision. Senseless appealing, where you know that there is no possibility of the batter being out, is against the spirit of cricket, is irritating to spectators, is time-wasting and is likely to lead to unnecessary bad feeling between the two teams. Leave this out of your game.

When things don't go your way

There will be plenty of occasions in your bowling career when things don't go your way. You will have plenty of catches dropped off your bowling, misfields that result in runs, snicks, edges and mishits that just evade the fielder's hands, slog shots off good deliveries that fly to the boundary. Wishing to show disappointment or even anger is a normal human reaction, but in the end does you or your team-mate no favours. Getting angry in such situations will almost certainly lead to you bowling poorly in the coming overs as the tension in your muscles and your thinking processes will almost certainly lead to a significant loss of rhythm.

Remember that we are all fallible human beings who are not perfect and who make mistakes. The fielder did not deliberately drop or misfield the ball and no one is more disappointed than he is. Do not let the emotion of the event have any effect on your bowling. Instead, remember that it can only take one delivery to turn things your way again. Grit your teeth and continue with your quest to out-think the batter.

Unfair tactics to avoid

If by chance any of the following should happen while you are bowling, stop, and if appropriate, apologise:

- Starting your run-up before fielders are in their assigned positions.
- Starting your run-up before the batter is ready.
- Bowling with flapping shirt sleeves.
- Bowling with a watch on your wrist – can be distracting to the batter, especially if the sun reflects off the screen.
- Bowling beamers – fast deliveries directed at the batter above the waist.

Comfort an injured batter

If you have hit the batter you are bowling to, do have the good manners to apologise, even if you believe it was the batter's fault. If he is badly hurt, go up to him and see if you can help.

Manners maketh the man

A quiet apology to your captain if you bowl a rank bad ball which is smacked to or over the boundary is proper. Likewise, the same will be appreciated by the wicket-keeper if you bowl an unintentional wide ball which goes for four byes.

Applaud a great shot

Another of cricket's delightful habits is to applaud a great shot by the batter. This may be tough to do if you are the affected bowler, but is a credit to your character.

Fielding

The importance of good fielding:

- There is no place in modern cricket for a poor or lazy fielder. Fielding can be a hardship for a hard-working pace bowler on occasions, but there is no excuse for lack of interest and enjoyment from the remainder.
- Three-quarters of all the active playing time you spend on the cricket field will be spent fielding. Therefore, it makes sense to spend at least as much time practising fielding as it does batting and bowling. If you do not enjoy fielding then you may as well give up the game at once and try some other sport.
- More progress has been made in the science and standard of fielding than any other areas of the game in the last twenty years. When a batter meets a team that moves in briskly with the bowler, always moves quickly to the ball, throws accurately, refuses to surrender easy singles or boundaries, he knows he is in for a hard day.
- You will be part of a team unit dedicated to the dismissal of the batsmen. You will be able to throw yourself wholeheartedly into a worthwhile mental and physical activity to the very best of your ability. Each fielder wants the ball to come to him; he wants to be involved as much as possible rather than being idle.
- If you are a non-bowling batter and have failed to contribute to the team total with the bat, make your contribution by denying the opposition as many runs as you can.

The part you play

Throughout your playing career, you will spend more time fielding than batting and bowling combined. Therefore, making yourself the best possible fielder you can be will not only increase your personal enjoyment of the game, but will make you a more valuable team member. Remember that

saving 20 runs in the field through your enthusiastic and athletic fielding is equal to scoring 20 with the bat.
You will get immense satisfaction from sprinting around the boundary to save a certain four, then after the save, with a fast flat throw back to the stumps. Likewise, a diving save in the covers which saves not only a certain boundary, but results in a run-out of a key batter, may be worth more to the team cause than any runs made or wickets you may have taken in the match to that point.

There is an old saying in cricket, as true today as when it was first uttered – "catches win matches". Teams that do not drop any catches in an innings very rarely lose the match. The message here then is to practise your fielding as much as you practise your batting and bowling. Do not neglect this essential skill.

Be ready to field anywhere

As you are just starting your cricket career, do not be in a hurry to specialise. Try out all the positions before you and your coach agree on your best position.

What is your best fielding position?

- Close catching: I have quick reflexes, good catching skills and an ability to concentrate for long periods. I have a calm temperament and do not seek the limelight.
- Infielder: I have a good turn of speed, agility, aggression, an accurate throwing arm and good hands.
- Outfielder: I have a strong throwing arm and good speed. I am confident in dealing with high catches.

How you can develop your fielding skills

- Learn the skills and methods of fielding; don't regard it as a minor part of the game.
- The fitter you are the easier fielding will become.

- Learn to concentrate. One way of doing this is to carefully study the batsmen. Ask yourself how you can help counter his strengths. If you believe you have seen something that your captain hasn't, tell him, but not to excess. Remember these practices are to help you stay alert and involved in the fielding effort.
- You should never force your captain to clap, wave, or call out to you to gain your attention if he wants to change your fielding position. Keep your eye on your captain and try to anticipate such moves.

Help to look after the ball

The following points will help prolong the shine and hardness of the new ball:

- Keep it off the ground as much as possible by relaying it back to the bowler in the air.
- If the ball is about to be returned from the deep by someone who does not have a strong throwing arm, go forward and catch his return before the ball bounces.
- If you are relaying the ball to someone who is looking into the bright sun, roll the ball gently along the ground. Obviously this method will not be right if the outfield is damp.
- Help keep the ball dry if the outfield is damp and if time permits, do your share of ball polishing.

Do not wander from your position

Do not move from where your captain has put you as he has put you in a certain position as part of his overall plan for the current bowler. In order to be sure of staying in position you need some sort of reference mark. Do not scratch a spot on the outfield with your spikes. Instead, look over the top of one of the sets of stumps to an object in the background to use as a reference mark for where you should be standing.

Keep a regular eye on the captain as he may want to move you to a new position without alerting the batters. If your captain wants you to move to a new position, move quickly so as not to hold up play.

Learn to anticipate

Practise anticipating a batter's shot and the direction it will travel after being hit. Many a run can be saved in this way, as well as many a difficult catch turned into a reasonably straight-forward one, by learning the art of anticipation. The good batter is always looking for the gap between you and the next fieldsman. You must also be aware of this gap and the moment the batter makes a move that indicates he is going for that gap, you should move to intercept the shot.

Be on your toes

Do this by walking forward as the bowler begins his run-up. This will help keep you mentally alert and ready to accelerate towards the ball if it travels off the bat in your direction. This is right for almost all fielding positions, even close catchers behind the wicket and the wicket-keeper when standing back to medium or fast bowlers. The fielders who must not do this are close catchers in front of the wicket such as short leg or silly mid-off.

Watching the ball or watching the bat?

Who should watch the ball or who the bat is often a matter for discussion among coaches and players. As a general rule you will be safe to remember the following guidelines -

Watch the bat if fielding:

- in the Slips, with the exception of First Slip
- at Point
- at Silly Mid-off and Silly Mid-on.
- at Short Leg, Leg Slip or Short Fine-leg

Watch the ball if fielding:

- at First Slip
- at Gully
- at Wicket-keeper
- at Backward Point

Watch the bowler, then the ball, then the bat if fielding:

- at Third Man
- at Cover-point
- at Extra Cover
- at Mid-off
- at Mid-on
- at Mid-wicket
- at Square-leg
- at Fine-leg

Infielding and outfielding

To give away unnecessary singles is an insult to you and to be avoided at all costs. You must make sure such mistakes are not repeated by making this goal a personal challenge if you are fielding in the infield. In the outfield you can seldom restrict singles but you can make sure they do not become twos or threes or even worse, boundaries.

Walk in as the bowler runs in to bowl. This helps with anticipation and makes sure your feet are moving and not planted in a stationary position. Stay light, on the balls of your feet with your weight forward in a slight crouch, ready to move quickly towards the ball. With time, you will learn to anticipate the batter's stroke, by noting the "shape of the shot", the batter's footwork and his arm movements.

Run as quickly as possible to the ball by estimating an intercept point and then travelling in a straight line to that point. Be prepared to get your body in the way of the ball, to do anything to cut off runs. One of the most frustrating things for your team-mates to observe is the ball going underneath the body of a fieldsman on its way to the boundary.

Always listen for guidance from your team-mates when intercepting or chasing after the ball. You may hear "bowler" or "keeper", alerting you to the fact that a batter is in trouble and you should throw to that particular end.

When fielding on the boundary do not move too far in from the boundary line before the ball is struck, as this will cut down the length of boundary you can protect. Also, if a catch is lofted in your direction, you will not want to have to turn and take the ball over your shoulder.

Good infielding is very much a team affair. Three or four high quality infielders all working together as a team will often pressure a frustrated batter into a fatal error of judgment.

Close catching

Slips specialists are vital to a team's success. This is especially so in junior grades of cricket where good slip fielders are a rarity. Good slip fielders are second only to the wicket-keeper in their importance to the team fielding effort. A key to being successful as a slip fielder is to believe that every ball is coming to you. Because of the high levels of concentration required, slip fielding can be mentally exhausting, so you need to learn how to relax between deliveries.

Close catching is a difficult skill and there is seldom an easy catch in close. Having a break from the slips through a run in the outfield can be beneficial and restore concentration levels when the player returns to his normal position.

Catches win matches

Good catching ability is vital for young cricketers. Note that you do not have to always practise catching with a cricket ball. Tennis balls are excellent for developing the skill of "soft hands". If your hands are too "hard" a tennis ball will bounce out. Using a softball and a softball mitt are also good practice as they lessen the risk of finger injuries.

Remember, that each catch you put down effectively increases the number of players against you. You need to get 10 wickets to dismiss a team, don't make it 15 by dropping five catches.

Use both hands

Always attempt to get two hands to the ball. Never catch with one hand unless it is absolutely necessary. The greater the surface area available to grip the ball increases the chances of making a successful catch.

Crossing the pitch

If you must cross the pitch between overs, do so right in the middle, where the ball does not usually pitch, to avoid causing damage that may affect the batters.

Fielder's appeals

It is unsporting for any fielder to appeal if he is in no position to judge. Mid-wicket might be quite justified in appealing for a run-out or a stumping but is in no position to appeal for a leg-before-wicket or a finely-edged catch to the wicket-keeper. Likewise, a slip fielder has no right to scream out an appeal for a close run-out at the bowler's end. When any member of the fielding team appeals, he is in effect saying to the umpire - "I really think, because I am in a good position to see, that the batter is out. Do you agree with me?"

Avoid the half-volley throw

Full-tosses and long-hops are equally easy for the wicket-keeper, but do not throw him, or especially the bowler, any half-volleys. No fielder wishes to bend unnecessarily, least of all the bowler who needs to be kept as fresh as possible. Half-volleys are easy to drop, even if they don't result in over-throws, and make the fielding side look most untidy. They can also cause injury, especially to fingers and shins, if not cleanly caught.

Hide your throwing arm from the batter

An experienced batter will quickly try and assess the foot speed and throwing capabilities of each outfielder. This needs to become a battle of wits between you and the batter. If you use the power of your throwing arm and your speed of foot only when absolutely necessary, you may trick the batter into taking a risky run which ends in a run-out for your team.

Overthrows

Be careful not to give away any unnecessary overthrows by hurling the ball at the stumps just because the batter is out of his crease. Many a batter will bait you into having just such a "brain explosion". So few of these throws result in run-outs, and so many in overthrows, that it is generally not worth the risk. So many quick singles turn into fives through this ill discipline on the part of the fielder.

Football or cricket?

Stopping the ball with your foot is a most untidy habit. It tells the batter and the spectators that you are a most unathletic competitor. Such a habit may be the form for "golden oldies" cricketers with their distended stomachs and their creaky knee joints, but not for a youthful cricketer like you.

High Catches

Once you have sighted the ball - and only then - get under it as quickly as possible as it is much easier to take these catches if you are stationary rather than on the move. It is up to you to decide which technique to use, the traditional English-style palms-up cupping of the hands or the more recent Australian-style reverse cupping of the hands. One method is not superior to the other. Use whichever you are most comfortable with.

Wear a cap

Many a catch has been missed in the outfield by the fielder suddenly being blinded by the sun in his eyes.

The dropped catch

Nothing is more certain, no matter how hard you practise, than that you will drop plenty of catches throughout your playing career. It is good manners on your part to apologise to the bowler and your skipper. An appropriate hand gesture will be sufficient.

A fair catch?

Occasionally there is doubt whether a fielder has caught the ball. As you will be playing in matches with nonprofessional umpires who will not have the benefit of replay technology, you need to help the umpires. You will know beyond all reasonable doubt whether you made the catch or whether the ball touched the ground just before your hands. If it is no catch or you are genuinely unsure, say so.

Back-up

When the ball is being thrown to either set of stumps, someone needs to back-up the throw to help prevent overthrows. Several of you may be able to do this, but it is the main responsibility of the fielder who is closest to being in an imaginary continuation of the straight line from thrower to the stumps. You must be close enough to the stumps to prevent extra runs being taken, but not so close as to be unable to get to a deflection or stop a high-bouncing ball.

Guard the stumps

There is nothing more frustrating than seeing a quick throw from one of the close-in fielders narrowly missing the stumps with no fielder there to stop the ball and remove the bails. This often affects the bowler, who will often stop and look at the action and not get back to the bowling end stumps ready to do his part in gaining a run-out.

Signal the umpire

If the ball beats you, as chasing fielder, to the boundary, signal the result to the umpire as he will probably be unsure whether it has crossed the boundary. Likewise, if there is uncertainty whether a skied shot is a four or a six, give the appropriate signal to the umpire.

Look after future pitches

Treat the entire pitch block (square) with care. Other pitches will be used after your match so do your utmost to avoid scarring their surfaces.

Wicket-Keeping

The importance of the wicket-keeper

He has the toughest job in the team and should be treated with the utmost respect by his team-mates. His is a highly specialised art and he is the élite of fielders. He catches more balls during an average day than anyone else and is never off duty, mentally or physically. He will finish each day of play more tired than any other player, with aching knees and back and sore fingers. Therefore, every member of the fielding team has an obligation to make his task as easy as possible. Remember, keepers are for throwing the ball to, not at!

Wicket keeping practice

Practise your wicket keeping as regularly as possible with all the bowlers in your team, so you can become totally familiar with their styles and variations. Talk to them about their wicket taking plans to better appreciate what they are trying to achieve. This practice is best done in open wicket situations rather than in the nets.

At net practice time, rather than become just another net bowler, work on your wicket keeping with a team mate away from the immediate vicinity of the nets

Standing up or standing back

Standing back to the faster bowlers and standing up to the spinners is self-evident, but what about the medium-pacers? Here are the pluses and minuses:

Standing up:

- denies the batter the breathing space to bat outside his crease.
- means the batter will be reluctant to advance down the pitch for fear of being stumped.
- makes it harder to catch fine edges.

- makes byes more likely to happen, especially to balls down the leg side.

Standing back means:
- byes will likely be fewer.
- catches will be easier, especially if the ball is moving about in the air.
- stumping the batter is no longer an option.

Inexperienced keepers usually stand too far back from the stumps and behind the middle stump. Instead, stand with your inside leg (nearest to the stumps) in line with, or just outside, off stump. Your distance back should be where you estimate the ball will carry through at about top of pad height.

Whatever you decide, don't get caught in "no-man's land", halfway between standing up and standing back.

Stay down

The most difficult thing for a young wicket-keeper is to learn to stay down until after the ball is pitched. Most will want to stand up too early, meaning that if the ball stays low or deviates sideways, the keeper will find it difficult to take the ball cleanly.

Your low start position is close to the height that you will likely catch the ball. This allows you to keep watching the ball and rest your hands on the ground.

Taking the ball

Every ball must be taken by the wicket-keeper in the mind - even if the batter hits it. Watch the ball, not the edge of the bat or the batter. Always "give" naturally with the ball - never push your hands towards the ball (snatching). Let the ball come to the gloves by waiting for it. Try to catch the ball in the middle of your stronger hand and then cover the ball with the glove on your weaker (non-catching) hand.

Pads are for protection

Pads should never be the primary means of stopping the ball. They are there for protection and as a second line of defence only.

Taking returns from the field

- All throws should be taken in the gloves. Never use the pads to deliberately stop the ball. Your pads are for protection and not to be used like the pads of a hockey goalkeeper.
- Always keep the stumps between you and the ball. Don't get in front of the stumps as this will reduce your chances of effecting a run-out.
- Always provide a target for the fielder by holding a hand up.

Move up to the stumps

Whenever the ball is likely to be returned to the batting end stumps by a fielder, make sure you move up to the stumps. In effect this means that unless the ball has been missed or left by the batter, you should move up to the stumps expecting the ball to be returned to you.

Be seen, not heard

Make keeping look easy, rather than sound easy. Don't talk to the batter unless he talks to you first.

Communicate with the bowlers

A word of encouragement to a hard working bowler is always welcomed. The bowler and the wicket-keeper can even work out traps for the batter together, especially if the batter is keen to move out of his crease at the ball. A slight prearranged variation in pace, flight or spin may tempt a batter out of his crease and present a stumping chance. The bowler and keeper should learn to communicate with subtle signals, unobserved by the batters.

The Captain

What makes an ideal captain?

The following are some of the characteristics of the ideal captain:

- He knows the game through reading, study and observation.
- He is familiar with the laws of the game and any special by-laws that apply to the grade or competition his team is playing in.
- He will have a good working relationship with his team coach and will seek his advice when unsure.
- He is cheerful and encouraging to all members of his team.
- He is a key contributor to the team with his personal performance with bat or ball or both. He may not be the best player, but through will-power and determination he will always strive to perform at the very best of his ability, especially if things are not going well for his team. He must have the biggest heart and be cheerfully prepared to take risks for the goal of ultimate victory.
- He will give praise when it is due and comfort when it is necessary, such as when a vital catch is missed or a duck is made.
- He will carefully manage the work-loads of his bowlers.
- He will understand the strengths and weaknesses of his bowlers and will set realistic and appropriate field placings, after consulting the bowler of course.
- He will lead by example and will not tolerate slackness or negativity by his team-mates.
- He will ensure by his deeds that the game is played in a positive and friendly spirit.
- He will be a welcoming host if he is the home captain.
- He will ask for other opinions from trusted team members, especially his vice-captain, if unsure of the correct tactics to use at any stage of the match.
- If he is himself a bowler, he will ensure that he bowls

himself when it is appropriate to do so and for the right number of overs, just as he would for any other bowler in the team. He must have the courage to take the ball himself, despite any potential criticism of his decision.
- He will ensure that his team members do not have to move too far between overs. Fine-leg to fine-leg, over after over, will not make a better fielder.

Here are some ideas how this can be achieved:
- Third man might move to long-on or mid-on.
- Fine-leg might move to long-off or extra cover.
- Square-leg might move to extra-cover.
- Third slip might move to mid-on or long-on.
- Mid-wicket might move to gully or backward-point.

If a right hand batter is batting with a left-hander and they change ends during the over, the following changes would be appropriate:
- Third man becomes fine-leg.
- Fine-leg becomes third man.
- Mid-on becomes mid-off.
- Mid-off becomes mid-on.
- Square-leg becomes point.
- Point becomes square-leg.

No-man's land
Remember when you are placing fielders that it is easier to run forward than to run back. If in doubt, place your fielder a little deeper than you might first have thought. It is most frustrating to watch a fielder desperately, but in the end unsuccessfully, trying to get back to a skied catch that falls just out of reach.

This is an aspect of the game that is most frustrating for the coach, and if not fixed, can add plenty of grey hairs to his head.

The toss

You have won the toss, do you bat or bowl first? Here are some tips to help you make your decision:

- Dry pitch - This can only deteriorate as the match progresses, so it may be an advantage to bat first when the conditions are most in favour of batting.
- An even covering of green grass - If you have a strong pace attack you may want to bowl first to take advantage of these seamer-friendly conditions. If the pitch is hard it should not deteriorate as the match progresses.
- An even cover of brown grass - This covering discourages seam movement, so most captains will bat first with this type of pitch.
- Strips of green grass running across the pitch - This indicates a pitch that is not totally flat and suffering from a condition known as "rolling bumps". This pitch will have variable bounce and will probably get worse, so it may be wise to bat first.
- Moisture in or on the surface of the pitch - This surface will assist bowlers in their attempts to swing, seam or cut the ball, so most captains will elect to bowl first, especially if there is a warm drying sun out.
- A damp outfield - Many captains will be keen to field first in these conditions as the dampness will slow the ball across the outfield, making fielding easier and run scoring harder. There will be an expectation that the outfield will dry out later in the day, making run scoring easier.
- A very hot day - This is usually a bat first situation. Having the opposition running around in the hot sun is physically draining and makes batting much harder

later in the afternoon, especially for the top order batters who will not have time to fully recover.
- A cloudy, muggy day - Here captains are often tempted to bowl first if they have quality swing bowlers in their line-up.

Whatever is the final decision, the captain should have consulted with his coach and senior team mates before making his decision. But in the end he must have the confidence to make the final decision if not everyone is in agreement.

Attack, attack, attack!

Never let the opposition batsmen settle down. Keep them continually on edge. Here are some thoughts on how to do this:
- Move a fielder after an odd number of runs have been scored to show the batsmen you are probing for their weaknesses.
- Regularly change the bowlers.
- Mix up the styles of your bowlers. For example have a left-armer bowling in tandem with a right-armer, or your fastest bowler with your slowest spinner.
- Consider starting an innings with one of your slow bowlers.
- Bring on a slow bowler just before an interval if they have been facing pace bowling for the previous half-hour.
- Bring on a non regular bowler for the last over before an interval.
- Many new batters to the crease are extremely nervous. The longer the fielding team can prevent such a batter from getting off the mark, the more nervous he will become. Batsmen on 49 and in the 90s can become equally nervous, so put them under pressure with appropriate field placings.

- Use attacking fields at the risk of "leaking" a few extra runs.
- Set fields that are appropriate to each batter in a partnership; they are most unlikely to be identically skilled.
- Be aware of the differences in the running between the wickets skills of each batter. The faster player will need to slow himself down to the speed of his slower partner, but many of them do not, and this can often lead to run-out opportunities.
- Never let an innings drift. If things are not going to plan, change the plan. For example, encourage a batter into a possible false stroke by leaving him a big gap square of the wicket, or bring a fielder into the eye line of the batter.
- Try and keep some overs available for your best bowlers towards the end of a limited over innings and make sure they bowl all their allowable overs in the innings. They are your best bowlers after all.

Appreciate your bowler's efforts

One of your regular roles is to make bowling changes. Often the bowler to be replaced will be reluctant to come out of the attack. Soften the blow with a "Well bowled" or "I'll give you a rest" as a courtesy and a method of thanks to the bowler being replaced.

Where should the captain field?

The most common fielding positions for a captain are first slip or mid-off. These two positions allow the captain to easily communicate with the bowler and wicket-keeper and to be close to the line of the ball when it is bowled. Fielding at first slip also has the advantage of having the captain in constant communication with his most important fielder, the wicket-keeper.

The declaration

There are many factors to consider when deciding to declare, such as:

- the size of the ground
- the pace of the outfield
- the time or overs remaining
- the runs to get
- your team's bowling resources
- the opposition's batting strength
- the weather and light

Even if you are concerned about the prospects of your bowling attack keeping a strong opposition batting line-up under control, there is no excuse for batting on so long that any target you eventually set is almost impossible. Such an approach will only cause bitterness in the closing stages of the game. There is a saying about declarations that has always been true - "To win matches requiring a declaration, you must be prepared to risk losing".

The home captain's obligations at the end of the match

These involve the following social courtesies:

- Be quick to congratulate the opposition captain if his team has won; be generous and modest if your team has been victorious.
- Thank the umpires and scorers. Don't take them for granted – they are essential to the game.
- Thank your supporters, and especially anyone in the provision of lunches or afternoon teas.
- Mingle with your team and the opposition in the time available after the match before everyone heads for home.

The visiting captain's obligations at the end of the match

The above list applies just as well to the visiting captain, but he might also consider thanking those responsible for the catering and asking for his appreciation to be passed on to the groundsman for the state of the wicket.

Umpiring and Scoring

Take an umpiring course

Even if you have no intention of becoming a regular umpire in your post-playing adult years, you should take an umpiring course at the earliest opportunity. There are two reasons for this. The first is that you will almost certainly be required to umpire your own matches at secondary school level. Indeed, some secondary school competitions do not permit adults to umpire. The second is that the best way to learn all you can about the laws of the game is through an umpiring course.

Bad officials spoil most games, but worse, biased or ignorant umpires can completely ruin a game of cricket. Don't allow yourself, while umpiring in your own match, to be caught out by ignorance of the laws when required to make a decision.

Make decisions based on what you see

Be guided by your catch-at-the-wicket decisions by noting any deflection off the bat rather than by any sound you hear. In other words, give your decision as out or not-out based on what you see rather than what you hear. There can be many reasons for sounds to occur which are not the result of the ball hitting the bat. Examples of these can include the ball edging the pad or a pad buckle, the bat hitting the pad or the bat scraping the pitch. All of these can confuse an inexperienced umpire and end in him making the wrong decision.

The LBW

Nothing causes young and inexperienced umpires more anxiety than having to rule on leg-before-wicket appeals. This is the one method of dismissal that causes the most potential for conflict between teams in junior cricket. You will have observed through television replays of how many times international umpires get these decisions wrong.

For example, in giving some incorrect "out" decisions they fail to notice that the ball would have bounced over the stumps, or that the ball pitched just outside the line of the leg stump, or that the batter edged the ball on to his pads, and so forth. Your job, however, is in many ways much easier as your decisions will not be subjected to replay analysis.

Making the right decision

The following tips may help you in making the right decisions:

- If in doubt, not out!
- Always pause before giving a decision.
- When appropriate, consult the square-leg umpire.
- Thoroughly learn the LBW law.
- Practise your umpiring during net practice sessions. Not only can you improve your feel for making the right call on LBW appeals, you can also work on adjudging front-foot no-balls and caught-behind nicks.
- Quickly get a feel for the amount the ball is bouncing. You can work with your square-leg partner on a simple set of hand-signals. When an appeal is made you can glance at your partner who can quietly signal to you whether or not the ball would have bounced over the stumps.
- Don't be bullied by the fielding team into giving an out decision. The loudness of the appeal is irrelevant. Be confident in your ability to make an unhurried but correct decision.
- At the bowler's end you should stand in line with the stumps and at a distance where you can look down over the top of the bails and still just see the batting crease.

Counting the number of balls in the over

This simple task is another that can cause young umpires potential embarrassment when lack of concentration causes you to lose count. If you have to call out to the scorers - "How many left in the over?"- you and your partner are not doing your jobs. Make sure you use an umpire's counter and always check with your partner that you agree when two balls are remaining in the over.

Changing your decision

You are entitled to change your decision provided you do so without delay. If you become aware that you have made a mistake after play has continued do not be tempted to "even things up" by calling, for example, a no-ball when none existed just because you missed an earlier one. A worse case would be to even up an earlier incorrect out or not out decision by treating a batter unfairly when a subsequent appeal is made.

Waiting for your signal to be acknowledged by the scorers

Never let the game go on until your signal has been answered by the scorers. On occasions you have to make two or even three signals involving just one delivery. As an example consider this case – a no-ball is bowled which is missed by the batter, resulting in the ball hitting the stumps and flying to the boundary. Firstly, after calling no-ball, you need to signal no-ball and wait for the scorers to respond. You then need to signal byes to tell the scorers the ball was not hit and again wait for that signal to be acknowledged. Finally you need to signal the boundary four and again wait for the signal to be acknowledged.

Standing at point

On occasions it is better to umpire at point rather than the expected square-leg. An example of this would be if you are having trouble seeing the crease lines because of the glare of the sun. As a courtesy, advise the fielding captain of your decision.

Do not obstruct the players

If the bowler asks you to move back (or forward) a little because of the style of his run-up, do so willingly without complaint. Stand absolutely still when the bowler is running in and delivering the ball so as not to distract the facing batter. If you are in the way of a bowler or fielder trying to stop the ball or take a catch, they have the right of way, so move out of their way.

It is the same for the square-leg umpire. You must be quick to move if the ball is heading your way and a fielder is trying to get to the ball. In doing so, however, make sure you keep your eyes on the crease line as you may be called upon to judge short runs by the batter or a run-out appeal.

Umpiring at square-leg, although needing less intense concentration than at the bowler's end, is not an excuse to totally relax. Much ill-feeling is caused in junior or lower grade cricket when a player umpire is not watching the play when an appeal is made for a stumping or a run-out.

To speak or not to speak

There are times when umpires should offer help, advice or instructions and others where it is best to remain silent. Here are some examples:

- When a new batter has taken guard, it is customary to tell the new batter how many balls remain in the over.
- If the batsmen are running on the pitch (grass) they must

be told to run off it. Often young batsmen run on the pitch because they have played all their previous cricket on artificial surfaces where there is no risk of damage being caused by the act of running between the wickets. This is not the case on grass pitches where the batter's studs and spikes can easily damage the playing surface.

- Likewise, if the bowler is running on the "restricted area" on a grass pitch he must also be warned. If he persists, then he is subject to the appropriate sanctions of the relevant law.
- Bowlers who follow-through in front of the umpire after they have bowled the ball need to be told that they are obscuring the umpire's view, thus preventing you from ruling on LBW or catches at the wicket.
- You do not need to explain not-out decisions to the bowler or the fielders after you have declined an appeal. Some umpires are in the habit of using hand-signals to indicate what the ball was doing when an LBW appeal is turned down. This is perfectly acceptable.

Some tips for the young scorer

This is a task you need to learn and become proficient at as you will be expected to contribute your time to this vital art at times throughout your playing career. However, it is true to say that modern computer technology is making the job of the casual scorer much easier. Scoring matches on laptop computers or smart-phones is becoming much more common and is likely to become the norm rather than the exception in future years.

Young scorers need to be aware of the following:

- Accurate scoring takes concentration. You need to carefully watch every delivery and learn to anticipate accompanying signals from one of the umpires.
- You need to acknowledge all umpire's signals, even

when what has happened is obvious to all. The umpire is required to keep signalling until the signal is acknowledged by the scorers, so don't cause a frustrating holdup in play by your lack of attention to this detail.

- You need to learn the standard score book symbols. Do not make up your own.
- You should verbalise what you are entering into the score book as it is unlikely you will be scoring by yourself. This will help avoid error. For example "3 to Barry" or "5 wides".
- You should get into the habit of checking with the other scorer at the end of each over that you agree on the match details. In particular the number of runs off the over and the total score. From time to time, when you have a spare moment, you should check the scores of the batsmen at the wicket and the totals of the extras.
- If you happen to be scoring when an innings is concluded, don't rush off to join your team-mates. It is your duty to check with the other scorer that everything adds up correctly and that all the finishing details are filled in.

Fair Play Code for Young Cricketers

The Players' Code

- Play for fun.
- Play by the laws of the game.
- Co-operate with team members and officials.
- Accept officials' decisions. Never argue.
- Work equally hard for your team and yourself - as both will benefit.
- Treat all players, officials and opponents as you yourself would like to be treated.
- Set a good example through your own behaviour, appearance and knowledge of the game.
- Applaud good play by both your teammates and your opponents.
- Have no interest in a "win at all costs" attitude.
- Never ridicule your team mates if they make mistakes. You could easily have been in their unfortunate position.

Cricket Terms

A cricketer is not really a cricketer until a knowledge of the history, tactics and laws of the game is acquired. What follows is a list of some of the most important terms in the game that a young cricketer may not yet know about:

all out - A batting team is all out when ten of the 11 batters are dismissed or retired out.

all-rounder - A player who is good enough to be selected for the team as either a batter or a bowler.

anchor the innings - He is the batter who nudges ones or twos while his partners at the other end play all the spectacular shots but get out. He is usually the batter in the team with the best defensive technique, who loves batting for long periods.

appeal - At least one member of the fielding team must appeal ("Howzat") to the umpires in order for a batter to be out.

arm ball - A ball bowled by a slow bowler without any spin on it. Bowled by a right-armer, it will either tend to drift slightly away from a right-handed batter or go straight on. Bowled by a left-armer, it will tend to drift in towards a right-handed batter or go straight on.

asking rate - The runs per over required to win the match by the team batting last.

averages - As a batsman your average is the answer to the number of runs you have scored divided by the number of times you have been dismissed. If you are a bowler, it is the answer to the number of runs scored off your bowling divided by the number of wickets taken. For a junior cricketer you are doing well if your batting average is above 20 and your bowling average is below 20.

backlift - The lifting of the bat before hitting the ball.

back-spin - The act of dragging the fingers down the back of the seam at delivery. It has the effect of keeping the seam upright, thereby increasing the chances of the ball swinging or seaming. For a spin bowler it helps flatten the flight, producing an unexpected increase in length for the batter.

ball tampering - An illegal act of changing the condition of the ball to gain an unfair advantage. Methods include scuffing the surface of the ball, picking or lifting the seam with the finger nails, or applying substances other than sweat or saliva to the ball.

bat pad - A close-in fielding position designed to catch out a batter, often after the ball has been edged on to the pads.

beamer - A ball that does not bounce and is directed (usually accidentally) at the batter's head. If bowled by a fast bowler it is a dangerous delivery and should result in an immediate apology from the bowler.

beaten - When a batter plays at the ball but fails to make contact, having been beaten by the pace, bounce, flight or sideways movement of the delivery.

blob - A duck, the dreaded score of 0 by the batter.

bouncer - Also known as a bumper. A ball which pitches short and passes the batter between chest and head high.

block - A defensive shot to stop the ball hitting the wicket.

blockhole - The part of the crease where the batter taps his bat. For the bowler it is the perfect place to aim the yorker.

boundary - The perimeter of the cricket field, usually marked by a painted line, a fence or a thick rope. It also refers to the scoring of a four or a six by the batter.

box - A groin protector worn by male batsmen and wicket-keepers.

break - The change in direction of the ball on pitching.

break the wicket - The wicket may be considered broken when at least one bail has been dislodged from the stumps by the ball, the batter, the bat, or a fielder's hand holding the ball.

If both bails have previously been dislodged, a fielder must pull a stump from the ground while holding the ball in the hand or hands holding the stump. The fielder can also, if he has time, replace one or both bails, before again removing them with the ball in hand.

bump ball - A ball that hits the bat and then the ground almost instantaneously. It is often mistaken as a catch and can cause difficulties for umpires.

bye - A run scored after no contact by bat on ball or by the ball on the batter's body.

carry your bat - Achieved by an opening batter who bats throughout the entire innings and is not out at the end after all his teammates have been dismissed.

caught behind - The batter is caught out by the wicket-keeper.

charge - A batter charges the bowler by moving briskly down the pitch to attack the ball.

chest-on - Refers to a bowler who delivers the ball with his back foot pointing down the pitch towards the batter.

chinaman - A wrist spinner bowled by a left-arm bowler which spins in towards a right-handed batter.

chinese cut - More commonly known as the French cut. This is a thick inside edge that just misses the leg stump and usually goes to the boundary at fine leg. Often results in a grumpy reaction from the bowler.

chin music - Fast bowling aimed at the batter's head.

chucker - A bowler who has an illegal action which results in him throwing rather than bowling the ball.

clean bowled - When a batter completely misses the ball and is bowled.

closing the face - Turning the face of the bat inwards towards the body, thereby directing the ball towards the leg side.

coffin - A name for the big rectangular shaped trunks that many senior cricketers use to keep their kit in.

collapse - The loss of several wickets in rapid succession.

corridor of uncertainty - The area just outside the off stump where the batter is unsure whether to play at the ball or leave it alone.

cover drive - Regarded as the king of batting strokes. Has a certain amount of snobbery about it as it is regarded as superior to any of the cross-batted strokes.

cow corner - A fielder who is placed on the boundary between mid-wicket and long-on to field or catch slog (agricultural) shots by the batsmen.

crease - There are three types of crease:

1. The popping or batting crease where the batter tends to stand in his stance. Also used by the umpire for judging whether the batter has made his ground when running between the wickets or when an appeal has been made for a stumping. Also studied carefully by the umpire to check whether the bowler has bowled a front-foot no-ball.
2. The bowling crease is an historical line which is not used in modern cricket. It used to be used for judging no-balls.
3. The return crease is used for judging whether a bowler has bowled a back-foot no-ball, a rare occurrence.

cut - The cross-batted strokes played between point and third-man. Also refers to sideways movement of the ball off the pitch when the bowler rolls his fingers across the seam.

dead ball - A ball from which no more runs can be scored or wicket taken.

death bowler - A bowler who specialises in bowling during the last few overs of a limited over innings.

declaration - When the batting side ends its innings before it has lost all its wickets.

dibbly-dobby - A bowler of slow medium pace who uses guile to trick batsmen into error.

dolly - A very easy catch which lobs in the air. A cause for great embarrassment to any fielder who drops one.

donkey drop - A very slow ball which was bowled high in the air with the intention of landing the ball on top of the stumps. Now an illegal delivery which is automatically called a no-ball as it is considered dangerous and unfair.

doosra - Bowled by a right arm off-spinner, it is the finger spinner's equivalent of a googly. It is bowled out of the back of the hand and spins away from a right-hand batter.

dot ball - A fair delivery from which no runs are scored. It is recorded in the score book with a small dot.

drifter - Bowled by a right arm off-spinner, it is a delivery that curves away from a right-hand batter. In effect it acts like a slow bowler's out-swinger.

duck - A score of 0 by a batter. Also known as a blob.

Duckworth-Lewis - A complicated mathematical formula to decide the result in a weather-affected match. Rarely used in junior grades of cricket.

economy rate - The average number of runs conceded by a bowler per over.

edge - An edge describes when the ball is slightly deflected by the edge of the bat.

extras - Runs not scored by the batsmen. These include byes, leg-byes, wides, no-balls and penalty runs.

feather - A very faint deflection or edge from the bat.

featherbed - A pitch which is particularly flat and easy to bat on and provides no assistance to the bowler.

finger spin - The type of spin bowling which has the ball propelled out of the hand by a flick of the fingers rather than a flick of the wrist.

fishing - A batter who aimlessly dangles his bat outside off stump away from his body.

five for - The taking of five wickets in an innings by a bowler.

flat track - A pitch with a very even surface which is easy to bat on.

flat-track bully - A term which describes any batter who only succeeds when conditions are in his favour.

flipper - A variation ball from a leg spinner which is pitched short but which skids on towards the batter, often catching him unawares, resulting in LBWs.

follow-on - A situation any batting team does not want to get into. It means that the team batting second in a two-innings match has failed to get within a certain amount of the team batting first and has to bat immediately for a second time. In junior cricket two-day matches the margin to avoid the follow-on is to be less than 100 runs behind the opposition.

four ball - A short or wide or half-volley ball asking to be smacked to the boundary.

friction - The grip of the ball on the pitch when it lands. The amount of friction slows the ball on landing and allows it to deviate sideways. A hard and fast pitch will have less friction than either a soft, wet surface or a dry and crumbling pitch.

full toss - A ball that reaches the batter below waist height without bouncing.

gardening - This is where the batter uses his bat to clear the pitch of debris or to repair small indentations in the pitch.

gate - The gap between bat and pad which often drives coaches to distraction. Batsmen who present this gap are often bowled "through the gate."

glance - The act of rolling the wrists and opening the face of the bat to use the pace of the ball to send it to the fine-leg fence.

golden duck - When a batter is out first ball of his innings for 0.

good length - The pitching length of the ball which results in the batter being unsure whether to play forward or back to the delivery. This is the desired target zone for all bowlers and must be practised relentlessly in the nets.

googly - A variation ball by a right-arm leg-spinner which turns in towards a right-hand batter. Also known as a "wrong-un".

grubber - A ball that hardly bounces after pitching. Also known as a "shooter".

half century - An innings of between 50 and 99 runs by an individual batter.

half volley - A ball that is a perfect length for driving. It pitches between a good length and a full-toss.

handled the ball - This is where a batter deliberately handles the ball when it is still in play. He can be given out on appeal. This often happens when a batter uses his hand to stop the ball rolling back or falling on to his stumps.

hat-trick - Three wickets taken in consecutive deliveries by a bowler. One of the most sought after achievements by a cricketer.

hawk eye - A network of cameras, computers and 3-D images to assist with the understanding of LBW decisions.

heavy ball - This is a delivery from a pace bowler which hits the bat harder and higher than expected.

hit the ball twice - This is where a batter deliberately hits the ball twice, then attempts to score runs. He will be given out on appeal. Note that it is allowable for a batter to hit the ball a second time to stop it hitting his stumps, provided he does not then attempt to score any runs.

hole out - A lofted shot which is caught on or near the boundary.

hook - A bold and risky cross-batted stroke played behind square-leg to a head-high delivery. It is risky because it is not possible to keep the ball down and failure to make contact can often lead to a nasty crack on the helmet. Not a stroke often played by young cricketers as such deliveries are usually called as no-balls because of height.

howzat - A contraction of the phrase "How is that?" Used by the fielding team for appeals.

hurry-up - A surprisingly fast ball designed to unsettle a batter who is getting on top of the bowling.

in-ducker - An inswinger that moves in to the batter very late in its path.

innings - The collective run-scoring efforts of the members of the batting team.

inside edge - When the ball hits the edge of the bat which is closest to the body.

inside out shot - A shot where the batter moves outside leg stump and hits the ball through the leg side.

in-swinger - A delivery that curves in the air towards the batter's body. The curve is the result of the different roughness (friction) of the two sides of the ball, which causes different air pressures on each side of the ball.

jaffa - A delivery that is too good for the batter. The batter ends up groping at thin air. Such a delivery often results in a dismissal.

jagging - A delivery that deviates sharply off the pitch.

knock - A batter's individual innings. "Great knock, mate."

leg-break - A delivery that turns, after pitching, from right to left from the viewpoint of the bowler.

leading edge - When the ball is mis-hit off the forward edge of the bat in a direction not intended by the batter.

leg before wicket (LBW) - This is where the ball first hits the pad or the batter's body and the umpire decides that it would have gone on to hit the stumps. The LBW law is somewhat more complex than explained above and needs to be thoroughly understood by young cricketers.

leg-bye - This is when the ball deflects off the batter's pad or body and runs are taken. The batter must have made a genuine attempt to hit the ball or must have been trying to avoid getting hit by the ball in order to take these runs.

leg-cutter - A ball that deviates (cuts) away from a right-hand batter after pitching. That is, it moves towards the slips. Achieved by dragging the fingers down the back of the ball and somewhat to the off-side (left).

leg side - The area of the pitch and outfield behind the batter's legs when he is taking strike.

length - The area on the pitch where the ball lands after being bowled.

lifter - A ball that rises awkwardly on the batter.

line - An imaginary straight line down the pitch which the ball follows after being bowled.

lolly or lollipop - A very easy ball for the batter to hit a boundary from.

long hop - A ball that is pitched short, which "sits up" and is very easy for a batter to hit to the boundary.

loop - The flight of the ball when bowled by a slow bowler. The bowler aims to get the ball above the batter's eye level to deceive him as to where the ball is going to land.

maiden - An over in which no runs which are scored are debited against the bowler, such as byes or leg-byes. However, this is normally an over where six dot balls are bowled.

manhattan - A bar graph detailing runs per over.

mankad - The act of the bowler running out a batter who has left the batting crease before the ball has been bowled. Not something that a young cricketer should get involved in as it is regarded as an unsporting act.

middle - The "sweet" spot on the bat. Also used to denote the guard taken by the batter and the area of the pitch and its surrounds where most of the action takes place.

military medium - Bowling that is in between slow and fast. Hard to score from and likely to bore everyone involved in the game. Try not to be regarded as this type of bowler.

milk - Where the batter's are effortlessly and without apparent risk able to score four or five runs an over. The batsmen are said to be "milking" the bowling

minefield - A pitch which is difficult to bat on. This is often caused by a pitch that has been uncovered during a period of rain or has been under-prepared for the match. The batter will have no certainty as to what the ball will do after pitching, with the ball often keeping very low or rising unexpectedly on the batter.

movement - Used to indicate sideways deviation in the air or off the pitch by a pace bowler.

nelson - A score of 111, either by the team or a batter. Considered to be unlucky, although no one knows why. Named after the famous British Admiral Lord Nelson.

nervous nineties - The period of anxiety for the batter as he approaches his century.

net run rate - This is a system to determine the winner of a match when bad weather prevents a result. It may also be used to separate sides in a competition who finish on the same number of points. It can be a complex series of calculations like the Duckworth-Lewis method.

new ball - This is a situation that can occur in matches of two or more days where the bowling team can request a brand new ball, usually after 80 overs have been bowled in the innings.

nick - A faint edge off the bat to the wicket-keeper.

night watchman - A tail-end batter who is promoted up the order to bat in place of a regular top-order batter for the last few overs of the day.

no-ball - A non-legal delivery, usually caused by the bowler over-stepping the batting crease. There are other causes of a no-ball, which all young cricketers must become familiar with.

not out - A batter who has not been dismissed or the umpire's reply to an unsuccessful appeal.

nudge - The act of a batter taking a risk-free single.

nurdle - The batter nudging the ball into gaps in the field.

obstructing the field - This is where the batter deliberately gets in the way of a fielder with the intention of preventing a catch being taken or a run-out effected.

occupying the crease - This is where a batter plays defensively with the purpose of staying in to help his team achieve a draw.

off-break/spin - A ball which spins in to a right-hand batter from off to leg (left to right).

off-cutter - A ball that deviates (cuts) in towards a right-hand batter after pitching. That is, it moves towards fine leg. Achieved by dragging the fingers down the back of the ball and somewhat to the leg-side (right).

off the mark - When the batter scores his first run(s).

off side - The side of the pitch to the right-handed batter's right when he is looking at the other end of the pitch.

on side - The same as the leg side.

on strike - When a batter is facing the bowling.

on the up - This where the batter makes contact with the ball before it reaches the top of its bounce. It is also known as hitting the ball on the rise. It is recognised as a rare skill, only achievable by the very best of batters.

openers - The two batters who start a new innings for the batting side.

opening the face - Angling the bat outwards in order to deflect the delivery on to the off side.

out - There are ten methods of dismissal. these are:

- bowled
- LBW
- caught
- run out
- stumped
- hit wicket
- timed out (very rare)
- obstructed the field
- handled the ball
- hit the ball twice

There is an eleventh way a batter can be recorded as out but it is not a method of dismissal. This is "retired out", not to be confused with "retired hurt" which is not recorded as out in the score book. Batters who retire out often do so in non-competition matches in order to give someone else a turn, especially if they have scored a century.

outside edge - When the ball hits the edge of the bat which is furthest away from the body.

outswing - When the ball swings away from the batter towards the slips.

over - A series of six consecutive balls by one bowler. Any no-balls or wides will mean the bowler will have to bowl extra deliveries to complete the over.

over pitched - A delivery of very full length that is easy for the batter to attack.

over rate - The average number of overs bowled per hour.

over-spin - Another name for top spin, where the top of the ball is rotated forward and the bottom backwards. Used by spin bowlers to try and gain bowled or LBW dismissals.

overthrows - Extra runs scored when the fielding team fails to stop a throw back to the stumps. Often caused by fielders failing to backup the stumps or from deflections of the ball off the stumps.

paddle - A sweep shot.

pair - When a batter makes 0 in both innings.

partnership - The total of runs scored by a pair of batters batting together.

pick - When a batter successfully predicts a variation in a bowler's delivery.

pie-chucker - A derogatory term for a bowler who is regarded as pretty hopeless.

pinch-hitters - This is a lower-order batter with a reputation for big hitting who is promoted up the order in the hope of getting some quick runs.

pitch - The bounce of the ball. Also used to denote the cut strip which the match is played on.

play on - When the batter hits the ball but it deflects on to the stumps and the batter is out. This dismissal is recorded as bowled.

plumb - When the batter is, obvious to all, out LBW. In other words, the batter may as well walk off before the umpire raises his finger.

pressure - To make life uncomfortable for the opposition.

pudding - A slow, stodgy pitch difficult to score freely on.

pull - A confident cross-batted hit to leg against a short ball. Less high risk than the hook as a skilled batter will be able to keep the ball down.

purple patch - A batter who can't stop scoring runs.

rabbit - A very poor batsman, regarded as an easy wicket for the bowling team. Sometimes has taken more wickets in their career as a bowler than they have scored runs as a batter. Is very familiar with scoring ducks.

radar - A bowler who sprays the ball all over the place is said to have "wonky radar."

retire - To postpone or end your innings. You postpone your innings if you have to retire injured or ill; you can resume your innings on the fall of the next wicket. You end your innings if you retire out.

return crease - Parallel white lines painted pointing down the pitch on either side of the stumps. A bowler must land his back foot inside these lines otherwise a no-ball will be called.

reverse sweep - A stroke which has become popular in recent years. Not recommended for young cricketers as the risk of embarrassment is high if you get it wrong. The stroke is played by going down on the back knee as if to play the sweep shot, but instead the hands are reversed and the ball is hit to the off side rather than the normal leg side.

reverse swing - Can be used by skilful pace bowlers when the ball is at least 40-50 overs old. The ball swings opposite to the expected direction. Not a skill to be mastered by young cricketers.

ring field - Fielders are positioned in a circular fashion around the batter with the object of stopping a quick single.

rip - A big-turning spinning delivery, more commonly bowled by wrist-spinners rather than finger-spinners.

rough - the area of the pitch that gets roughed up and loosened as the game progresses. The main culprits here are the bowler in his follow-through and the batter when starting off on a run. This rough is often a tempting target for spin bowlers in the later stages of matches.

run-chase - This is the stage late in the game when the match situation has been reduced to a certain number of runs required in a certain number of overs.

run-rate - This is the average number of runs scored per over.

runner - A player who is called upon to run for an injured batter. He must wear exactly the same protective gear as the injured batter and must stand where directed by the umpires.

scrambled seam - When the bowler releases a wobbling ball that is unlikely to swing or land on the seam.

seam - The ridge of stitching that keeps the two halves of a cricket ball together. The seam is important in the physics of swinging the ball and in enabling a bowler to achieve deviation off the pitch.

shocker - Often refers to an appallingly bad decision by an umpire. Can also refer to a particularly bad spell by a bowler.

shoulder arms - This describes the motion of the batter lifting his bat high above his shoulders to keep it and his gloved hands well away from the ball.

shooter - A ball that hardly bounces. Also known as a grubber.

side-on - Refers to a bowler who delivers the ball with his back foot pointing parallel to the bowling crease.

sight screen - Unfortunately a rare feature in any grade of junior cricket. Used to give the batsmen a distraction-free view of the red cricket ball against a white background.

sitter - The easiest possible catch. A source of major embarrassment to a fielder if he drops one.

sledging - The fielding team's way of upsetting a batter's concentration through certain often personal comments directed at him. It is often described as a form of mental disintegration. It is not needed in junior cricket; leave it to the seasoned adults. Do your talking with bat and ball.

slip cordon - The area between the wicket-keeper and gully where fielders are placed for the sole purpose of catching edged catches.

slog - An undignified stroke designed to give the ball an almighty whack. To call a batter a slogger is regarded as an insult.

slower ball - The most commonly used variation used by pace bowlers, designed to keep batsmen guessing and playing too early at the ball.

snickometer (snicko) - An audio device that picks up the faintest sound of bat on ball.

spell - The number of consecutive overs bowled by one bowler before he has a rest.

square - The collection of pitches in the middle of the cricket ground. In order to stay on side with the groundsman, do not dare to make any scratch marks on this treasured rectangle of green grass.

sticky wicket - A drying wicket that is very difficult to bat on.

stock ball - A bowler's regular delivery. A ball that is designed to deny a batsman the chance to either score runs off, or to let through to the keeper.

stonewall - To bat with excessive caution. Has no place in limited over or junior cricket grades.

stumps - The collection of three upright sticks, that along with the bails, make up the wicket at each end of the pitch. Also used as a term by umpires to announce the end of a day's play.

strike(r) - The batter facing the delivery is said to be on strike or the striker.

strike bowlers - The bowlers in a bowling team expected to take the majority of the wickets. They usually open the innings.

strike rate - The average number of runs scored by a batter per 100 balls or the average number of balls per wicket for a bowler.

sweep - A high-risk stroke which is difficult to master and not recommended for batters under the age of fourteen. The batter goes down on one knee, in full knowledge that the ball could hit him in the face, and plays the ball with a horizontal sweeping motion towards square-leg.

swing - A ball that curves through the air rather than seaming, cutting or spinning off the pitch. The swing is achieved by having the seam at angle to the flight of the ball or from uneven damage to the ball, resulting in a sideways push of the ball from the more shiny side to the less shiny side.

tailender - A player who bats in the lower part of the order, generally numbers 9, 10 and 11. They are not noted for their batting ability.

tea - An afternoon break of no more than twenty minutes.

throwing - To deliver the ball illegally with the arm flexing at the elbow at more than the allowable limit, which is currently 15 degrees. Throwing allows a pace bowler to achieve extra pace and a spinner to achieve extra spin. A bowler who is confirmed as a thrower (chucker) through slow-motion video analysis, will need remedial action from a specialist bowling coach to fix the problem.

tie - Occurs when the team batting last in a two-innings match is dismissed for one run less than the score which would have won the game. In other words, when both teams end up with the same total of runs over two innings. In one day games there cannot be a draw, so the team batting second does not have to be dismissed for it to be a tie.

toe - The bottom edge of the bat.

ton - A century (100 runs or more) by a batter in a single innings. One of the most sought after achievements by a cricketer.

top-spinner - Where the top of the ball is rotated forward and the bottom backwards. Used by spin bowlers to try and gain bowled or LBW dismissals.

toss - The pre-match ritual of the home team captain tossing a coin and the visiting captain calling "heads" or "tails" to decide which captain has the right to decide whether to bat or bowl first.

track - Another name for the pitch the match is being played on.

twelfth man - A substitute fielder. If called into action he can field in any position but may not bat or bowl. In junior cricket the 12th man on the list is often allowed to be either a non-batter (he is allowed to bowl) or a non-bowler (he is allowed to bat).

two-paced - A wicket that has become worn, allowing some deliveries to shoot through low, while allowing others to rear up off a length.

turn - Change of direction from the pitch. The bottom of the ball, on contact with the pitch, moves sideways.

turning wicket - A pitch that is spinning a great deal.

twenty20 - The recently developed 20 overs per innings form of the game which is taking the cricketing world by storm. A match that only lasts three hours and is well-suited for attracting families and fringe cricket supporters to the ground. Also known derogatorily as "hit and giggle."

V, the - The angle between mid-off and mid-on which the batter aims to play the ball within, especially in the early part of his innings, to lessen his risk of getting out.

wagon-wheel - A circular graph for each batter showing where he has scored his runs.

walking - The act of a batter agreeing he is out without needing to wait for an umpire's decision. Regarded as one of the most principled (sporting) decisions a cricketer can make.

wicket - The stumps and bails together make the wicket. Can also be used to refer to the pitch that the game is played on.

wicket maiden - An over in which a bowler takes a wicket and also concedes no runs off the bat or through wides or no balls.

wide - A ball that is considered too far away from the batter to allow him to play a normal cricket stroke. This definition will vary depending on the type and level of cricket being played.

wrist spin - The type of spin bowling which has the ball propelled out of the hand by a flick of the wrist rather than a flick of the fingers.

wrong-un - The Australian term for a googly.

yips - A derogatory term which refers to a bowler, usually a left-arm spinner, who loses the ability to land the ball with any consistency and ends up sending down an embarrassing mixture of long-hops, full-tosses and half-volleys. Believed to be a psychological condition, it has ended a surprising number of careers.

yorker - A full pitched delivery aimed at the batter's feet or the base of the stumps. Designed as a surprise delivery which aims to take a wicket.

zooter - A variation on the flipper. A ball that is said to "zoot" along, barely rising off the pitch.

Cricket Speak

The following is a list of amusing cricket sayings suitable for young cricketers to know about, but not to be used against the opposition in the heat of the battle.

Batting sayings

"Have a go, ya mug!" This means to forget about your average and get on with it.

"You're a bunny!" An easy wicket for the bowler he is facing.

"Feel free to use the bat!" When a batter repeatedly plays at and misses the ball.

"Well left!" When it is obvious to everyone that the batter has been completely bamboozled by a great delivery.

"Leave the rubbish!" Where a batter appears to be doing his best to get out despite the poor standard of the bowling.

"My grandmother could have hit that!"

"The bat's not for decoration you know!"

"You can use the whole bat you know!"

"Gone!"

"It's not a bloody test match!" Also known as "Get on with it!"

"Run'em up!" According to the coach, the batsmen aren't running fast enough between the wickets.

For the bowlers

"He's a pie thrower!" This refers to a particularly unskilful bowler who should have lots of runs scored off him before the real bowlers come back on.

"Slow down, we can't see it!"

"The faster you bowl, the further they go!" A common phrase used after a tearaway fast bowler has had a rank bad ball dispatched to the boundary.

For the fielders

"He couldn't catch a train!" He's just dropped another sitter.

"You couldn't catch it with a bucket!"

"Good arm!" A boundary fielder with a very weak throw.

"Go the ball!" You mentally will it towards the boundary.

For the umpires

"It would have missed two sets of stumps!"

"What about the no-ball?"

"You can't give that out, you've given nothing all day!"

"Get your ears checked, grandad!"

"Come on, stick your finger up!"

For the uneducated spectators

"Who's winning?"

"Why's he wearing a crash helmet?"

"Have you had half-time yet?"

"A draw! How can it be? They've been playing for two days!"

"He's got a 100, why doesn't he give someone else a go?"

"It's just a game!"

"He bent his back that over!"

"He cut him in half!"

"That's what happens when you turn blind!"

"He was beaten outside the off stump!"

"Got him neck and crop!"

"He chanced his arm and it's come off!"

"That one's gone straight down his throat!"

"Another coat of varnish and we would have had him!"

"Good nut!"

"They can't buy a run!"

"He's going through a bit of a trough!"

"He's been taken to the cleaners!"

"Catches win matches!"

"He's hung the washing out!"

After the match

"Either side could have won."

"Cricket was the winner on the day."

"Play one ball at a time, and play each ball on its merits."

"We snatched victory from the jaws of defeat."

"We snatched defeat from the jaws of victory."

"It's back to the drawing board."

"We need someone to step up to the plate."

"Man of the match - Duckworth Lewis!"

Resources for young cricketers

Useful Websites

www.cricinfo.com - the home of cricket on the internet.

www.blackcaps.co.nz - the New Zealand cricket website.

www.pitchvision.com - highlighting the latest in cricket technology, plus tips and advice from professional coaches.

www.youtube.com - hosts dozens of coaching videos.

www.maverickscricket.com - for tips and advice from professional coaches.

Recommended Coaching Books

Tom Smith's New Cricket Umpiring and Scoring - the definitive guide to the laws of cricket.

Bob Woolmer's Art and Science of Cricket - the best coaching book in the last 25 years.

Ian Pont's The Fast Bowler's Bible - compulsory reading for any budding young fast bowler.

Ken Davis and Frank Pyke's The Cutting Edge Cricket - tips and techniques from 38 legends of Australian Cricket.

Alan Pearson's Cricket: Training and Conditioning for Cricket - a complete cricket training programme.

8208508R00077

Printed in Great Britain
by Amazon.co.uk, Ltd.,
Marston Gate.